the Laundry Book

CONTENTS

INTRODUCTION

Who We Are and Why We Wrote This Book • **9**

CHAPTER 1

Let's Get Started • **15**

CHAPTER 2

An Overview of Laundry Products • **23**

CHAPTER 3

Sorting Your Dirty Laundry • **33**

CHAPTER 4

The Art and Science of Stain Removal • **41**

CHAPTER 5

Washing Basics • **51**

CHAPTER 6

Drying Basics • **73**

CHAPTER 7

Getting the Wrinkles Out • **83**

*"I can remove any stain,
just give me a pair of scissors!"*
—Lou

This book is dedicated to Lou Scricca.

Thanks to him, we are not just dry cleaners;
we are experts!

He was the foundation of our cleaning knowledge,
expertise, and dedication to quality.

We've passed on your invaluable lessons
with anyone willing to learn.

All our love,
Your son and grandson (Jerry and Zach)

First published in 2024 by Rock Point, an imprint of The Quarto Group,
142 West 36th Street, 4th Floor, New York, NY 10018, USA
(212) 779-4972 www.Quarto.com

10 9 8 7 6 5 4 3 2 1

ISBN: 978-1-57715-449-5

Digital edition published in 2024
eISBN: 978-0-7603-9108-2

Library of Congress Control Number: 2024933383

Group Publisher: Rage Kindelsperger
Editorial Director: Erin Canning
Creative Director: Laura Drew
Managing Editor: Cara Donaldson
Cover Design: Beth Middleworth
Interior Design: Beth Middleworth and Rebecca Pagel
Illustrations: Jessica Durrant (pages 10, 36, 102, 108)

Printed in China

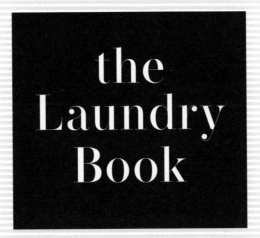

the Laundry Book

The Definitive Guide to Caring for Your Clothes and Linens

Zach Pozniak and Jerry Pozniak

ROCK POINT

CHAPTER 8

Hanging and Storing Your Clothes • **93**

CHAPTER 9

What Do Dry Cleaners Do? • **101**

CHAPTER 10

The Laundry Cycle, Rinse and Repeat • **113**

CHAPTER 11

The Joy of Clean Clothes • **121**

CONCLUSION

Your Laundry Journey • **125**

Appendices • **128**

Index • **204**

Acknowledgments • **207**

About the Authors • **208**

WHO WE ARE AND WHY WE WROTE THIS BOOK

THE LAUNDRY BOOK

The goal of this book is to make the never-ending chore of laundry easier. We believe that having access to easily digestible and correct information is extremely important, so you can solve your laundry problems the first time around. But who are we, and why should you trust us?

We are Jerry and Zach Pozniak, a father-and-son team and third- and fourth-generation dry cleaners, who are passionate about providing science-backed and thoroughly tested solutions for all things related to caring for and cleaning your clothing, bedding, and textiles.

Jerry started his career as a photographer after graduating from the School of Visual Arts. His stepfather, Lou Scricca, had been in the dry-cleaning business since 1958 and asked him to help him out in the family dry cleaners for a few years. These "few years" quickly turned into four decades of fabric-care expertise. Lou's father had been in the dry-cleaning business, along with his father and two brothers, which made Jerry the third generation "in the business." Jerry has literally cleaned millions of garments.

Zach took a slightly different path that ended in the same place. He studied mechanical engineering at Binghamton University, and then he pursued a career in construction management, focusing on high-end residential and hospitality build-outs. Jerry asked Zach to consider working with him, and after a few years of persuasion, he joined the dry-cleaning business in 2018.

Together, Zach and Jerry own and operate Jeeves New York, a luxury dry-cleaning company based in New York City, which focuses on cleaning high-value and specialty garments that require more love and attention than a typical piece of clothing.

Jeeves, which was established in London in 1969, came across the pond to New York City ten years later and is the only international, luxury dry-cleaning company. While Jerry and Zach own the New York business, there are Jeeves shops in seventeen cities across the globe, with a high concentration in Asia and the Middle East. Jeeves has a Royal Warrant as "the" dry cleaner to the Prince of Wales. For many years, Jeeves had cared for the clothing of Prince Charles (now King Charles) and his family, including Princess Diana and their children, William and Harry.

Why does a luxury dry cleaner exist? Well, one of our favorite responses to this is, "Would you take your Ferrari to a Ford dealership?" The same is true for those one-of-a-kind pieces that are bespoke, couture, vintage, and heirlooms. What separates Jeeves from all other dry-cleaning firms is unsurpassed attention to detail and decades of experience.

Jeeves New York has taken care of every textile you can imagine, hand-cleaning vintage couture Balenciaga dresses that were displayed in the Louvre in Paris, as well as restoration of textiles for the Metropolitan Museum of Art, Cooper Hewitt, and the Fashion Institute of Technology. The largest textile cleaned by Jeeves was a ninety-by-thirty foot (27 by 9 m) felted-wool-and-silk artwork by the Dutch artist Claudy Jongstra, which hangs in Lincoln Center.

While Jeeves' focus is luxury, couture, and bespoke items, we have clients who rely on us to take care of their entire wardrobes, including restoration of family heirlooms, preservation of wedding dresses, and the cleaning of everything from a child's beloved stuffed toy to a favorite The Clash T-shirt from 1979.

Unfortunately, 2020 was an incredibly difficult year for dry cleaners. Usually, dry cleaners and laundry services are recession-proof businesses—as Jerry's dad used to say, "There are always dirty clothes to clean." However, that proved not to be the case during a global pandemic. Jeeves' revenue dropped 85 percent overnight, and we were left to figure out a way forward.

We decided to shift our focus to sharing the decades of garment-care information in Jerry's head with the rest of the world. After many failed attempts to produce "how-to" guides, we were finally welcomed by the online cleaning community as a trusted source of laundry information, thanks to the rise of short-form social media. Initially, our focus was to-the-point stain-removal video guides, which quickly expanded to all garment care—everything from the best way to store your sweaters to preventing, and correcting, yellow underarm stains.

And now, we have compiled all our cleaning information in this book. It is an all-inclusive "field manual" on how to care for your clothing, bedding, and textiles. Don't worry; this prologue is the only time you'll read anything about us. There is no additional fluff about who we are in this book; it is designed to help you get laundry done right the first time.

This book is not designed to be read cover to cover, but to be skipped through, so you can find the information you need. We hope you enjoy it and find it valuable.

We believe clean clothes are a human right.

CHAPTER 1

LET'S GET STARTED

A Brief History of Laundry • **16**

Laundry around the World • **18**

Where to Do Your Washing and Drying • **20**

This book will teach you everything you need to know so that you can do your laundry right the first time, which will save you time. We share our tricks and tips as professional dry cleaners with decades of experience cleaning millions of garments, from simple T-shirts to $250,000 Chanel couture gowns that were worn at the Met Gala.

What we are not going to do is recommend specific brand names of laundry detergents, laundry products, and washing machines and dryers. If we did, this book would be obsolete before it was printed. You can find recommendations for products and appliances by visiting the following websites:

- The Clean Club (thecleanclub.com)

- *The New York Times* Wirecutter (nytimes.com/wirecutter)

- Consumer Reports (consumerreports.org)

- Good Housekeeping Institute (goodhousekeeping.com/institute)

These websites provide unbiased information and reviews of all things laundry. Some have advanced search functions, so you can compare products to see what works best for you and your household.

A Brief History of Laundry

When did we start washing our clothes?

The first record of washing clothes dates to 2800 BCE, with the Sumerians. Laundry was cleaned by beating the clothes with rocks at a river, as the flowing water would carry away stains and odors.

Laundry was done by the entire family in ancient cultures. It was hard work and took days to complete. Dirty clothes were added to water tanks in communal wash houses and stomped on with bare feet. Grains, soap, and sometimes urine were used to remove stains.

During medieval times, cleanliness was not a priority, so washing development did not continue. People thought the plague was carried in water, so bathing and clothes washing were done infrequently. The preferred method of washing was boiling clothes and then beating out the dirt with sticks.

The seventeenth century brought the invention of the *valcha*, or washboard, which was a huge technological leap for laundry. Soap was produced in Spain and Italy from olive oil and ash, making the process much more productive. Laundry was time-consuming and labor-intensive during this period and was primarily taken care of by women, as it was considered a part of their domestic responsibilities.

Manual washing tubs and rudimentary washers were made in the late 1700s to help cut down on labor. The heyday of manual washing machines was in the 1800s—paddles and rods with hand cranks enabled agitation, and rollers with cranks enabled wringing of clothes to remove as much water as possible before air-drying. Laundry could take multiple days to do, depending on how much needed to be washed.

Nathaniel Briggs patented the first metal washboard in 1797 in the United States. The metal, ridged surface made doing laundry more efficient, offering better results for scrubbing and stain removal. This style of washboard is still being used today.

The invention of small electric motors fueled the advancement of electric washing machines in the 1900s, which automated a previously labor-intensive chore. As washing machines and dryers became more common in households in the late-nineteenth and twentieth centuries, it can be noted that these devices had implications for women's liberation and gender roles. The amount of time required to take care of laundry was shortened from days to hours.

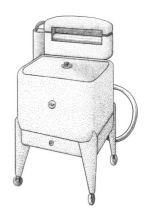

Time-saving machines gave women opportunities that were not open to them in the past, such as education, employment, and joining political movements. This is a complex subject, and the washing machine may have played a small part in a very large aspect of a societal transformation.

Laundry has become easier, but it is still time-consuming. Our book will help guide you, so it becomes less of a chore.

Laundry around the World

While it may not be obvious, the task of laundry is done differently across the globe. Access to running water and electricity, paired with the cost and infrastructure required for appliances, demand creative solutions for this chore. Here are some key differences spanning the continents.

Automatic washing machines are a luxury in developing countries, where most people still use washboards paired with running water and a laundry soap bar to clean their clothes. In a pinch, you can wash your clothes in a sink or a bucket. We have washed our clothes in a hotel sink when traveling.

In areas where space is an issue, such as Europe and Asia, washing machines are usually installed in the kitchen, and clothes are dried on a clothesline or drying rack. In some homes, the laundry appliance does double duty and washes and dries in the same machine.

At times, in India, people do the washing by hand, beating items against carved rocks or concrete blocks. After washing, they are rinsed, wrung out by hand, and dried in the sun.

Instead of clotheslines, in Singapore, laundry is hung on bamboo poles that extend out from the balconies of apartments; it is a very efficient way of drying clothes, considering the lack of space and hot, breezy climate.

FUN FACT
Eighty percent of US households have a washing machine as of 2022.

Germans have regulations about noise, so loud music, drilling, and noisy washing machines cannot be used during the *Ruhezeit* (quiet time), which is from 10 p.m. to 6 a.m. daily and all day Sunday. So, if you don't own a noise-free washing machine, you cannot do laundry on Sunday.

Here are some statistics from a Nielsen report from 2015 that break down how laundry is done around the world:

Washer & Dryer
Laundromat
Handwash & Clothesline Dry
Outsourced

ASIA PACIFIC

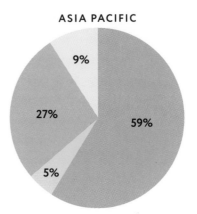

9%
27%
59%
5%

LATIN AMERICA

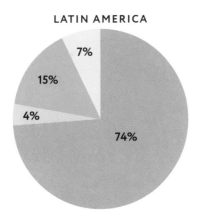

7%
15%
4%
74%

EUROPE

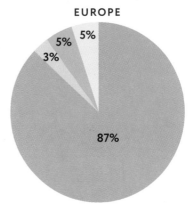

5% 5%
3%
87%

NORTH AMERICA

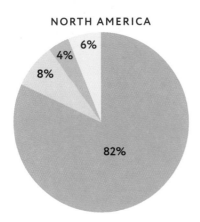

6%
4%
8%
82%

AFRICA AND THE MIDDLE EAST

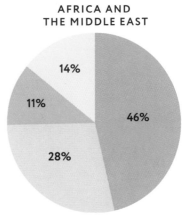

14%
11%
46%
28%

Where to Do Your Washing and Drying

No matter where you live, you will need to find a way to wash your clothes, towels, bedding, and other textiles. If you live in a house or apartment, you may have your own laundry space, or you may share a laundry room with others in an apartment building.

or you will need to go to a laundromat. When traveling, the bathtub or sink may become your laundry room. No matter where you are or what you have at your disposal, our book will help you keep your items clean.

Basic home laundry rooms will have an automatic washer and dryer and, perhaps, a table to fold your laundry. If you are using a communal laundry room in an apartment complex or dorm, or have to go to a laundromat, you may see a room that looks much different from a home setup.

Laundromats and communal laundry rooms will have multiple washers and dryers. Some may have super-large-capacity machines to wash and dry large items, such as comforters and washable rugs that you cannot wash in smaller home machines. Even if you have a laundry room in your home, you may need to venture out to a laundromat occasionally to wash bulky and large items.

Shared laundry rooms will have a payment system to use the washers and dryers. Older machines will require coins for operation, whereas modern machines will allow payment with credit cards, reloadable payment cards, or smartphone apps. They may have large folding tables, vending machines for detergents, and televisions for entertainment.

Laundromats may also offer "wash and fold" services to take care of your laundry for you. The fee for these services is by the pound; stained items may not get pretreated, and items may get lost, but it does save time.

In the United States, there are laundromats that have gyms, cafés, restaurants, bars, remote work pods, and, in Brooklyn New York, even a speakeasy hidden behind a door that looks like two clothes dryers. Who knew?

Luckily, washing machines and dryers have come a long way since their inception. In the coming chapters, we will do a deep dive into them, as well as discuss their environmental impact and what is in store for the future.

CHAPTER 2

AN OVERVIEW OF LAUNDRY PRODUCTS

Laundry Detergent • **24**

Laundry Boosters • **28**

Liquid Fabric Softener • **30**

Dryer Sheets • **30**

Scent Beads • **31**

W alking down the cleaning-product and laundry-detergent aisle of your local grocery store may make you feel overwhelmed with choices. As someone once said to Jerry, "Too many choices is no choice at all." Tide, Persil, Gain, Arm & Hammer, Dreft, Woolite, Dropps, Kirkland, Seventh Generation . . . How do you pick one?

Laundry Detergent

We have some disappointing news: we are not going to tell you which are the best detergents, as manufacturers release new products and update old recipes frequently. If we told you the best ones today, months from now there may be something better. To find the best laundry products for you and your family, we recommend checking these websites that provide transparent information alongside up-to-date reviews:

- The Clean Club (thecleanclub.com)

- *The New York Times* Wirecutter (nytimes.com/wirecutter)

- Consumer Reports (consumerreports.org)

- Good Housekeeping Institute (goodhousekeeping.com/institute)

THE GOOD STUFF

What you need to know is that high-quality laundry detergents will do a much better job of removing soil and stains than others. Price does not directly correlate to better cleaning performance, as we have tested expensive laundry detergents that have underperformed compared to others that are half the price.

Now for a quick chemistry lesson. Detergents are made up of a few key ingredients that clean your clothes and remove stains.

SURFACTANTS: These are the most important cleaning ingredients. They loosen and surround soil and stains, allowing water, or other cleaning solvents, to wash them away.

BUILDERS: These are chemicals that help surfactants do their job by softening hard water. If you are in an area with hard water, these are especially important.

ENZYMES: These are what we like to call the superheroes of detergents. Specific enzymes target certain stains, such as blood, grass, food, and oil. Look for protease, amylase, and lipase in the ingredients. Enzymes in detergents work similarly to how enzymes in our digestive tract process and break down food: they take large complex molecules and convert them into smaller molecules, making them easier to digest, or in this case, wash away.

ANTI-REDEPOSITION AGENTS: These prevent the dirt and soil suspended in the wash water from going back onto your clothes.

BLEACHING AGENTS: These whiten and brighten fabrics. Examples are sodium percarbonate and hydrogen peroxide.

FRAGRANCE: This is added to give your laundry a scent.

Laundry detergents that do not do a great job of removing stains will leave out key ingredients, such as enzymes, builders, bleaching agents, and anti-redeposition

Shop Talk ONLINE DIY RECIPES

Many of the DIY laundry-detergent recipes that are featured on social media use bar soap and a few other ingredients in such scant amounts that they are ineffective compared to high-quality products. We made a few DIY detergents, and the results were poor. We are all for DIY, but when it works.

agents. From our laundry-detergent testing, the products that scored the worst for removing stains did not contain enzymes. Look for these when buying detergent, especially if your laundry has a lot of stains.

Some of the eco-friendly laundry detergents that pride themselves on sustainable packaging and plant-based and natural ingredients are performing better than previous iterations, but as of this writing, none have surpassed the offerings from the top consumer brands. We have hope that these underdogs will be the top dogs in the not-too-distant future.

POWDERS, LIQUIDS, SHEETS, AND MORE

Prior to laundry-detergent powders, soap bars, such as Fels-Naptha, were used with washboards. In 1907, the German company Henkel invented Persil, the first widely available laundry-detergent powder and the first to use sodium perborate as a bleach. Procter & Gamble (P&G) followed with Dreft powder in the 1930s and Tide in 1946.

Liquid detergents became popular in the 1960s, and this form of detergent became mass-marketed with the release of Tide Liquid in 1984. Liquids gained popularity, as they were less messy than powders and consumers found them convenient.

Eco-friendly brands have been spearheading alternative forms of detergents, such as solid tablets, sheets, and powders (going full circle). These brands are rethinking packaging to make them recyclable or less wasteful.

As of this writing, here is the breakdown of the laundry-detergent market:

LAUNDRY DETERGENT

- Liquid
- Powder
- Pacs
- Sheets
- Other

2%

6%

20%

48%

24%

ALL ABOUT LAUNDRY PACS

You may know these better as Pods, a term trademarked by P&G, so we will refer to them as "pacs." Pacs were invented by various companies, so the jury is still out regarding who should be credited with this innovation, though they were first brought to market by P&G under the banner of Tide in 2012. Other brands market them as pacs, capsules, discs, and tabs.

What is unique about laundry pacs is that they are easy to transport, contain a single dose, and reduce spills, messes, and overuse of detergent. Detergent makers can separate key ingredients in pacs that may counteract each other in traditional liquid or powder form to make a detergent that is more effective at removing soil and stains. The casing that holds the liquid detergent is made of a water-soluble material, usually a polyvinyl alcohol.

There are some concerns about the release of microplastics into the wastewater stream from the dissolved pac casing or film. Detergent manufacturers say that the release of microplastics from pac casings is less than the shedding of microplastic fibers from synthetic clothing during washing. This is a highly debated topic, and there is not a clear consensus or conclusive data about the subject currently.

Pro Tip **HOW TO DISSOLVE LAUNDRY PACS**

If you are having problems with your laundry pac dissolving, we recommend putting it in a sock or mesh bag. This will help break down the film through mechanical action (page 55). Or you can run the pac under water for a few seconds before placing it in the machine.

The downsides of laundry pacs are safety concerns, including ingestion by children, which was addressed by using child-proof containers with locking lids, as well as the casing potentially dissolving if handled with wet or damp hands.

If you are using pacs, we recommend that you place the pac in the tub of the machine and then add your laundry. The film that holds the laundry-detergent ingredients together dissolves once it comes into contact with water. Our tests have shown that agitation, or mechanical action (page 55), allows the film to dissolve more quickly than just being in contact with water. Agitation is the rubbing action of the items being washed either by tumbling in a top-loading machine or with fins in a top-loading machine. Do not place the pac in the compartment labeled "detergent"; that should only be used for liquid or powder detergents. Some high-end washing machines are now equipped with a compartment for laundry pacs.

Laundry Boosters

Now that you're an expert on laundry detergent, let's talk about supplemental products. These are products you can add when washing your clothes to enhance the results. Using high-quality detergent will negate the need for boosters, but they will help if you have a specific problem. For brand-name versions of these products and reviews, consult The Clean Club (thecleanclub.com).

AMMONIA: Household ammonia can be added to increase the effectiveness of detergents, but it needs to be handled with care and never mixed with chlorine bleach, as it will produce harmful toxic fumes. If you are using a high-quality detergent, adding ammonia will never be necessary.

BAKING SODA: Also known as sodium bicarbonate, this is used to soften hard water, which will brighten whites and help remove odors.

BORAX: Also known as sodium borate, this is a naturally occurring mineral compound. In laundry applications, it increases the effectiveness of detergents, softens hard water, and removes some stains.

CHLORINE BLEACH: Also known as sodium hypochlorite and calcium hypochlorite, this is used to sanitize garments and remove stains. For as long as we can remember, chlorine bleach was lauded as the best way to whiten clothing. While there is some truth to this, we do NOT believe it is the best way to whiten clothing, as it usually does more harm than good. Extreme caution is needed when working with chlorine bleach around colored items, as it can cause damage. Chlorine bleach's greatest strength is as a disinfectant to kill mold, bacteria, and viruses. Wear gloves and old clothes when handling chlorine bleach and never use it around or mix with ammonia; it creates harmful toxic fumes. We do not recommend the use of chlorine bleach unless you need to sanitize your laundry, and we have instructions on how to do this on page 67.

OXYGEN BLEACH: Also known as sodium percarbonate, this can be added to your laundry as a color-safe alternative to chlorine bleach. When it comes in contact with hot water, it creates hydrogen peroxide and soda ash (sodium carbonate), which whitens and brightens your clothing. Powdered oxygen bleach works best in hot water (140°F, or 60°C). See the Soaking section on page 65 for our recommended method when using oxygen bleach.

VINEGAR: White vinegar has a variety of uses in the laundry room. It can be used as an odor remover, a DIY alternative to soften clothing, and a stain pretreatment for acid-based stains. When used in the washing machine, add it to the fabric softener compartment and make sure you select the Softener option for your washing machine cycle. In a pinch, or if you don't have white vinegar, lemon juice is a satisfactory alternative.

WASHING SODA: Also known as sodium carbonate and soda ash, this is used to enhance the effectiveness of laundry detergent, soften hard water, remove some stains, help with odor reduction, and brighten whites.

Shop Talk FABRIC SOFTENER

It's best to think of fabric softener like conditioner for your hair. It does not have any cleaning functions, but it can help protect fibers and add softness. Fabric softeners provide softness and protection by coating the surface of a fabric with chemical compounds that are electrically charged, causing threads to "stand up" from the surface, thereby imparting a softer and fluffier texture.

Liquid Fabric Softener

Fabric softener was a staple laundry product for generations, as cotton garments used to be much stiffer and scratchier; however, softeners have lost popularity in recent years due to improvements in fabric comfort and a shift from natural fibers to synthetics.

There are many pros and cons when using softener, so it's important to understand how it works and how to use it properly before making your decision. Essentially, fabric softener coats fabrics with what is, effectively, a lipid, or fatty, layer that makes your clothes feel softer. This fatty layer builds up over time, which attracts dirt and soil that is difficult to remove.

Fabric softener causes natural fabrics to become less absorbent and less breathable, which is not great for undergarments, bedding, and towels. Fabric softeners can clog your washing machine, coat the drum of your dryer and dryer sensors, and make fabric more flammable. For these reasons, we do not recommend using fabric softener for most clothing. However, fabric softeners do have benefits when used properly for animal- and protein-based textiles such as wool, cashmere, and silk.

Dryer Sheets

We also are not fans of dryer sheets, which are squares of polyester fabric (polyester is plastic) coated with what is essentially fabric softener. During drying, the sheets release the softener, which reduces static cling, imparts a softer "hand feel" to your clothes, and adds fragrance. This coating of softener will make your clothes and towels less absorbent and may affect fabric texture and irritate your skin.

While not perfect, we love dryer balls, as they can reduce static cling and somewhat reduce wrinkling of your items during drying. Dryer balls allow for better air circulation around the items you are drying and keep items in the dryer separated. Contrary to some opinions, dryer balls do not reduce drying time, according to our testing. If you want to add a touch of scent to your laundry, you can add a drop or two of essential oil to your dryer ball to impart a pleasant fragrance.

Scent Beads

One of the newest supplemental laundry products currently on the market is scent beads, which entered the market in 2011. Scent beads are in-wash scent boosters that are designed to provide long-lasting freshness to laundry loads.

The primary technology in scent beads is perfume, as well as perfume capsules. Perfume capsules work like tiny scent bubbles that deposit on fabrics, survive the wash and dry cycles, and burst when friction is introduced, releasing fragrance (think when wearing a garment, using a towel or sheet, moving around in clothing, or other interactions with fabrics).

To use scent beads, add them directly to the tub of your washing machine before putting in your laundry. They are designed to work in all machines, for all wash cycles, and for all fabrics. Most scent beads are made of fragrance, dye, and polyethylene glycol (also known as PEG), a water-soluble polymer used as a carrier for perfume technology.

It is important to remember that scent beads are completely optional and provide only scent; they do not clean.

CHAPTER 3

SORTING YOUR DIRTY LAUNDRY

Check the Garment Care Labels • **34**

Check Pockets, Unbutton Buttons, and Zip Up Zippers • **35**

Pretreat Stained Items • **35**

What Does "Like Items Together" Actually Mean? • **36**

Why So Many Different Loads? • **38**

Before you wash your laundry, you need to sort it. Yes, this will take some up-front effort, but in the long run, it will save you time. Sorting is easy because there is one simple rule: "like items together." At Jeeves, and hopefully at every dry cleaner and professional laundry, each garment is sorted into "like" loads. It would be dangerous to clean a delicate silk blouse with heavy wool coats. (The weight of the wool coats during the dry-cleaning wash cycle could damage the delicate silk fabric.)

Check the Garment Care Labels

Of course, you need to check the garment care labels to make sure that everything you want to wash can be washed. It is a good idea not to wash items with care labels that read:

- Do not wash

- Dry clean only

- Leather method only

- Spot clean only

If you have garments that say any of these things on the label, set them aside and refer to chapter 9 (page 101). You can also reference The Garment Care Label Guide on page 129 to help you decipher what the symbols mean and to help you sort your laundry.

FUN FACT

A dry cleaner's worst nightmare is an "ink load." This is when a foreign object with concentrated amounts of pigment and dye, such as a pen or lipstick, is washed and bleeds onto clothing. Correcting an ink load is extremely labor intensive and often unsalvageable.

Check Pockets, Unbutton Buttons, and Zip Up Zippers

As you are sorting, check all the pockets of every garment. If lipstick, lip balm, pens, or candy are in a pocket, it could ruin everything in that wash load. Lipstick can melt in water and pens can release ink. Tissues in pockets can be a problem, as they fall apart and leave tissue lint on everything.

Unbutton all buttons on your items; otherwise, during washing and drying, too much stress may be put on the button thread, causing loose or missing buttons.

Zippers should be pulled up to prevent snagging of other garments from the zipper teeth.

Pretreat Stained Items

Another good sorting tip is to pretreat stained items as they are being sorted and added to the hamper. Simply put, select the correct pretreatment for the specific stain, pretreat it, allow the stained area to dry, and then put the item in the laundry basket. You can pretreat a stain for up to one week. If you did not do this ahead of time, separate out the items with stains, as you are going to want to pretreat them before washing. This is because the longer a stain treatment sits on a stain,

the better it will work. In chapter 4 (page 41), we discuss stain-removal techniques, which, if accomplished beforehand, will save you time in the long run. Pretreating removes more stains during washing, so you won't have to wash something twice, which not only saves time but will also give you better results.

Pro Tip INVEST IN A LAUNDRY SORTER

Having a laundry sorter is a huge time-saver. We like one that is on wheels and has three removable bags. You can label each bag to your preference, but we have labeled ours with:

- White/Light Colors
- Dark/Bright Colors
- Delicates

What Does "Like Items Together" Actually Mean?

In broad categories, the first sort should be by color, making piles of light- and dark-colored items. You don't want to wash a pair of dark denim jeans with your white towels, as the indigo will bleed during washing, making your towels a nice shade of light blue.

Another, less obvious, reason to keep light and dark items separate is lint. Lint is an inevitable byproduct of the washing and drying process that can cause a real headache when not accounted for. For example, if you dry your dark clothes with your white terry towels, expect lots of white lint from the towels on everything dark. Also, white clothes will often look gray and dingy due to dark lint from dark clothing. If this happens, you can spend hours with a lint brush, or you can rewash the linty clothes, which should solve the problem.

Trust us; despite sounding like a cliché, this happened to us when a red sock went rogue and hid underneath a load of white sheets, which are now pink.

After some basic sorting of light colors from dark colors, you can lean into your laundry obsession by separating further. Doing this will help your clothing last longer, as each of these categories have very different wash and dry cycles:

- Delicate items

- Gym and athletic wear

- Towels and linens

- Items for a normal cycle, such as socks, T-shirts, undergarments, and basics

- Heavy outerwear and skiwear

- Badly stained items

- Things you wash infrequently

- Everything else, such as denim, new garments that may bleed, and even washable shoes

For those who do not have the time, space, or means to run half-a-dozen loads of laundry, we recommend separating lights and darks and worrying less about garment weight. While there will be a few drawbacks, mostly during the drying cycle (wrinkled cotton T-shirts being one example), this will still help save time and money.

Pro Tip HOW NOT TO LOSE SOCKS

Keep a box of safety pins near your laundry basket, so when you are adding socks to the basket, you can pin the toes of each pair together and never have an "odd" sock. You can also put your socks in mesh laundry bags (lingerie bags) to keep them together. Mesh laundry bags are also good for washing delicate items to protect them.

Why So Many Different Loads?

There are many benefits to separating "like items," but most importantly, it will reduce unnecessary stress on your clothing and prevent them from degrading prematurely. Keep in mind that the washing and drying process is usually the most aggressive, invasive, and harmful experience in a fabric's life, so proper sorting can reduce the severity of long-term damage.

One of the main reasons sorting is so important is for the drying cycle. Laundry dries depending on how much water is in each item after spinning (or extraction). Natural fibers, such as cotton and linen, absorb more water than synthetic fibers used in workout clothes, and more water in an item equals a longer drying time.

For example, when you remove your gym clothes from the washing machine, they may almost feel dry, and they are, as they did not absorb much water at all, whereas

Shop Talk SYNTHETIC FABRICS

Synthetic fabrics are made from plastics and absorb a minimal amount of water. This is why gym clothes can "wick" away perspiration—the moisture does not get absorbed by the fabric but works its way from the inside to the outside where it evaporates, making you feel cooler than having a soaking-wet cotton T-shirt against your skin during your workout. Sweaty workout wear should be hung up and air-dried before being placed in the laundry basket. Sometimes we want to bury our stinky workout stuff at the bottom of our laundry, but this causes the clothes to become smellier, and in some cases, mold may grow. Yuck.

cotton towels and sheets will feel very wet and be heavy, as they have absorbed a lot of water. So, if you mix cotton clothes with your workout clothes, the workout items will be dry long before the cotton items. Imagine what would happen if you mixed your workout clothes with cotton towels!

By keeping "like items" together, they will get cleaner during washing and will dry with fewer wrinkles, as all the garments are drying at the same rate.

Many dryers have specific settings depending on what you are drying. The controls may have a setting for towels and sheets, cotton garments, workout clothes, delicates, and more. They have been programmed to use a heat setting and will measure residual moisture, which will lessen dry times and save you time and energy. We talk about drying and settings in chapter 6 (page 73).

CHAPTER 4

THE ART AND SCIENCE OF STAIN REMOVAL

Simplifying Stain Removal • **42**

How to Remove Stains • **45**

Stain-Removal Products and Tools • **46**

How to Keep Stains from Ruining Your Stuff • **48**

What to Do If You Get a Stain While Out and About • **48**

W|ater is the best stain remover for common stains, which is good news for you, as doing laundry uses water.

Simplifying Stain Removal

Stain removal can be an incredibly overwhelming and daunting task, as almost everything we humans come in contact with can cause staining. Our goal is to distill a seemingly infinite number of stains into a few manageable groups. The good news is that just about every stain falls into one of four categories—greasy/oily, particulate, enzymatic, and oxidizable—which means there are really only four stain-removal processes you need to understand to remove most stains! Once equipped with this information, you will have more knowledge than even some dry cleaners.

GREASY/OILY STAINS

Greasy/oily stains are most often caused by cooking oils, food products, machinery, and cosmetics. They often appear slightly translucent and will creep along the fibers, making a cross shape with a blurred or soft edge. Food and drink stains without an oil component will dry with a hard edge or "ring" in comparison.

To remove these stains, you will need to use a surfactant, a staple ingredient used in cleaning detergents as the primary or secondary ingredient. The most common

examples of surfactants are dish soap and laundry detergent. Surfactants have a unique molecular structure that allows them to attach, surround, and pull away grease and other types of stains from the surface or fabric. A surfactant molecule looks a bit like a tadpole. The head of the tadpole loves water (hydrophilic), while the tail hates water (hydrophobic). So, the tail attaches itself to the soil—grease in this case—while the head, attracted to the polar water molecules, pulls the soil away from the fiber thanks to the help of water.

PARTICULATE STAINS

Particulate stains are created by a multitude of different minerals and chemical components. While this may sound complicated, we're referring to things such as dirt, mud, soil, and clay. These dirt particles can be hard to remove from clothing due to their metallic bonds.

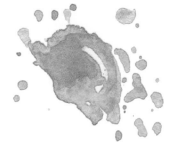

To remove these bonds, you will need to use something known as a builder (page 25). Common builders are baking soda (sodium bicarbonate), washing soda (sodium carbonate), and borax (sodium borate). They are compounds with the power to neutralize calcium, magnesium, aluminum, and other metallic elements responsible for particulate stains. Once the bonds between the molecules are gone, the soil and mud can be easily removed from the fabric with regular washing.

ENZYMATIC STAINS

Enzymatic stains occur when proteins, sugars, and fats in food or other substances bond with the fibers in clothing. This bonding can happen through a process called "denaturation," which occurs when heat, acid, or agitation causes the protein molecules to unravel and bind to the fibers. Most food stains, blood, grass, and urine are examples of enzymatic stains.

Simply put, once these large molecules have bonded to the fibers, they are difficult to remove and can lead to discoloration or yellowing of the fabric. Fortunately, most high-quality stain-removing products include enzymes such as proteases, amylases, and lipases, which break down specific staining molecules. Once the large molecule stains are "digested" by the enzymes, they are much easier to remove with the help of a thorough cleaning. Check the ingredients of your favorite stain-removing spray to ensure enzymes are included.

OXIDIZABLE/BLEACHABLE STAINS

Oxidizable/bleachable stains are usually the brightest and, often, most challenging stains to remove because their resiliency can require patience and multiple efforts to fully remove them. Common examples of oxidizable/bleachable stains include berries, tea, juice, and red wine.

The tricky part is that while removing the physical stain is not difficult, as most are water-based and rinse out easily, once dry, the stain's color is often left behind, which requires a color-correction process known as "bleaching." Before we talk about bleach, you should know that oxidizable stains are caused by a chemical reaction called "oxidation"; this reaction is when oxygen is introduced to a stain and causes it to change color—the identical reaction when an apple turns brown after it is cut. Most oxidizable stains are caused by normally harmless invisible compounds that turn into a brown pigment called "melanin."

To remove oxidized stains, you need to use chlorine or oxygen bleach, but please do not use chlorine bleach unless it is absolutely necessary.

SPECIAL STAINS

Special stains include, but are not limited to, wax, gum, paint, crayon, ink, and most types of oil-based makeup. Each of these stains is usually difficult to remove, and results from at-home remedies are limited because these stains are mostly hydrophobic and do not rinse out with water. Luckily, your dry cleaner should excel at removing these stains.

COMBINATION STAINS

Most stains do not fall into one specification, so it's important to understand that multiple consumables and processes may be needed for stain removal. An easy example of this would be a Bolognese sauce (tomato sauce with meat), which has greasy, enzymatic, and oxidizable components.

How to Remove Stains

Before you refer to The A-to-Z Stain Removal Guide (page 136) for removing the most common stains, here are some general stain-removal tips:

- The sooner you treat a stain, the more likely it is to come out.

- Always check the care label to see if your garment can be washed at home. Do not try these processes on "dry clean only" pieces.

- Testing the pretreatment you plan to use on a stain on a hidden area of your garment prior to treating a stain is highly recommended to avoid possible issues.

- Higher water temperatures during washing will usually work better at stain removal. We recommend starting with cold water and then moving up to warm and hot water if the first process does not work.

- Adding washing boosters (washing soda, baking soda, and borax) to the tub of your washing machine increases the pH of the wash water and almost always allows a stain's pretreatments and detergents to work better. Our recipe is two-parts washing soda, one-part baking soda, one-part borax, and one-part sodium percarbonate (oxygen bleach). Add ¼ cup (30 g) of this booster recipe to the tub of your washing machine.

- There is a limit to what can be achieved with at-home stain removal. Certain stains are nearly impossible to remove at home (ink, gum, smoke odor, makeup), and the same goes for caring for certain types of fabrics (rayon, acetate, wool).

Just like anything in life, there is a time and place to call in a professional for help (see chapter 9 on page 101).

Stain–Removal Products and Tools

We cannot emphasize enough the importance of pretreating stains, as doing this will save you a lot of time and effort. There is nothing more disappointing than seeing that those stains you thought would come out in the wash remain . You are going to need a few things to tackle stain removal at home like a professional dry cleaner; if you follow our recommendations, you will soon be a stain-removal expert.

- Dish soap (we think Dawn works best) or laundry detergent

- Washing and/or baking soda

- Cleaning vinegar (at least 20%) or white vinegar

- Powdered oxygen bleach (sodium percarbonate)

- 3% hydrogen peroxide

- Rubbing alcohol (isopropyl alcohol)

- All-purpose stain-remover spray with enzymes

- Soft-bristle brush

- Clean terry towels or washcloths

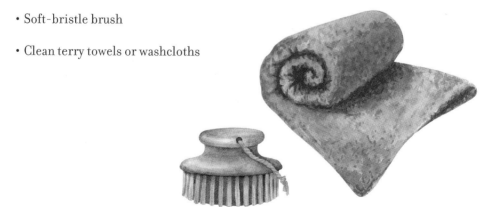

Once you have these items, use The A-to-Z Stain Removal Guide (page 136), which will give you DIY step-by-step instructions to remove almost any stain you encounter. To see the best stain-remover products that you can purchase, please go to:

- The Clean Club (thecleanclub.com)

- *The New York Times* Wirecutter (nytimes.com/wirecutter)

- *Consumer Reports* (consumerreports.org)

- Good Housekeeping Institute (goodhousekeeping.com/institute)

STAY SAFE: NEVER MIX THESE PRODUCTS TOGETHER

Some of the stain-removing products listed opposite should never be mixed with one another or with other cleaning products, as they can result in dangerous reactions. Here's our guide:

CHLORINE BLEACH (SODIUM HYPOCHLORITE) AND AMMONIA: Mixing chlorine bleach with ammonia can produce toxic chloramine vapors, which can cause respiratory problems and irritation.

CHLORINE BLEACH AND ACIDS: Mixing chlorine bleach with acids, such as vinegar or lemon juice, can release chlorine gas. Chlorine gas can cause respiratory distress and other serious health issues.

CHLORINE BLEACH AND RUBBING ALCOHOL (ISOPROPYL ALCOHOL) OR ACETONE (NAIL POLISH REMOVER): Combining chlorine bleach with rubbing alcohol/acetone can produce chloroform and other toxic compounds. This mixture can cause dizziness, nausea, and even organ damage.

HYDROGEN PEROXIDE AND VINEGAR: Mixing hydrogen peroxide with vinegar can create peracetic acid, which can irritate the eyes, skin, and respiratory system.

BAKING SODA (SODIUM BICARBONATE) AND VINEGAR: While these two substances are often used for cleaning, combining them in a closed container can lead to a rapid release of carbon dioxide gas, causing pressure to build up and potentially leading to an explosion.

How to Keep Stains from Ruining Your Stuff

Professional dry cleaners know that the sooner you start the stain-removal process, the better. We recommend that once you see a stain, use the procedures in The A-to-Z Stain Removal Guide (page 136) as soon as possible. Even if you do not wash your item right away, pretreating the stain will make the odds of removal much better.

We do not recommend going to the internet for stain-removal techniques. We have spent years developing the guidelines in the appendix and testing them to make sure they work with products you can purchase at supermarkets and drugstores. Many of the stain-removal tips found online do not work or will damage your clothes. Take it from us: we have seen our share of tears at Jeeves from clients who damaged garments by using online stain-removal tips.

What to Do If You Get a Stain While Out and About

First, don't panic! You cannot do much while you're out, but you can do more harm than good. Don't let well-meaning friends or restaurant staff ruin your clothes.

Sparkling or club soda does not remove stains any more than water does. The

carbonation has no magical properties; otherwise, dry cleaners would use it by the gallon. Plain water will do the same as sparkling. We recommend that you ask for a clean, dry, absorbent towel or napkin and blot the stained area to absorb as much of the liquid from the stain as possible. You can use a bit of plain water to dilute the stain, but only blot it—please, please, please do not rub. Rubbing could chafe the fabric, damage the surrounding dye and spread the stain even more.

Don't use the hand soap in the bathroom; this will only make the stain worse because you will have residual soap as well as the stain. There is no easy way to rinse the soap from the garment, and you don't want to rub the area with toilet paper.

If you get an oil stain from, let's say, dipping bread into olive oil, and it is making you crazy, you can try to sprinkle a small amount of cornstarch or baby powder on the stain. Let it sit on the stain for about ten minutes and then brush it off. This may work as the cornstarch/baby powder can absorb oil. This is also a great technique if you get an oil stain on suede or leather.

Treat the stain as soon as you get home, or if the garment is "dry clean only," bring it to your favorite cleaner sooner rather than later.

CHAPTER 5

WASHING BASICS

Top-Loading vs. Front-Loading Washing Machines • 52

Loading the Washing Machine • 52

Parts of a Washing Machine • 53

Adding Products and Selecting a Cycle • 55

Start Your ... Washing Machine • 61

Post-wash Inspection • 63

Handwashing • 63

Soaking • 65

Sanitizing: Hot Water and Chlorine Bleach • 67

When Not to Wash • 68

Washing Machine Problems and Maintenance • 69

Automatic washing machines are a magnificent invention, which makes "doing" laundry much easier than in the past. If you have never used a washing machine, there are a few things you need to know before you start.

Top-Loading vs. Front-Loading Washing Machines

Washing machines are either top-loading or front-loading. Top-loading machines have a door on the top, and front-loading machines have a door in the front. While top-loading machines are still the most common type of washer (making up about 60 percent of the residential market), front-loading machines are gaining in popularity. There are pros and cons of both:

- Top-loading machines are larger, less expensive, and can soak your garments; however, they provide less cleaning power and use more water.

- Front-loading machines are the choice of all laundry professionals and dry cleaners because they provide the best stain/soil removal and use minimal amounts of water; however, they generally have less capacity and are more expensive than top loaders.

Loading the Washing Machine

So, how much laundry should you put into the tub of the machine? Remember to follow our instructions in chapter 3 (page 33) about checking all the pockets, unbuttoning buttons, zipping up zippers, pretreating stains, and sorting before this step.

Never fill the basket more than three-quarters full on each machine. We know you want to get out of the laundry room as quickly as possible, but filling the washing machine more than this will limit mechanical action, and guess what? Stains, soil, and odors will not be removed, so you will waste more time rewashing everything.

PARTS OF A WASHING MACHINE

Now that you understand the differences between machine types, it's time to learn about your machine's main components.

LOADING DOOR: The loading door, whether on top or in front, allows you to put your laundry into the tub.

TUB: Also referred to as the basket, drum, or wheel, the tub holds the items to be washed.

AGITATOR: You'll notice that inside some top-loading machines, there is something that resembles a corkscrew or, perhaps, fins. This is called an agitator, which introduces mechanical action (page 55) during the washing process. These are more common in older top-loading machines and are being phased out by appliance manufacturers. Front-loading machines do not have an agitator; they rely on the tumbling of the items in the basket for mechanical action.

CONTROL PANEL: The control panel helps you make your wash cycle selections.

PRODUCT-COMPARTMENTS DRAWER: This is where you add your cleaning products.

There are a few more parts of the washing machine, but we'll get to them later in the Washing Machine Problems and Maintenance section on page 69.

Pro Tip   DO THE HAND TEST

When loading your laundry in a front-loading machine, there should be about 6 inches (15 cm) of space between the top of your laundry and the top of the tub; or the width of your hand.

CHECK THE GARMENT CARE LABELS

You should also check the garment care label to see what the manufacturer of those jeans you want to wash says. Here are the washing symbols you will find on the care label and what they mean (refer to The Garment Care Label Guide on page 129 for more information on these care labels):

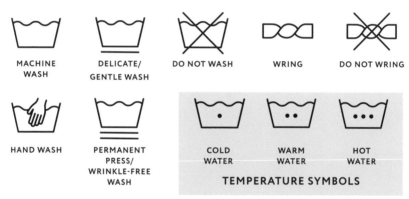

Pro Tip   WHAT CAN BE WASHED?

Garments made from cotton, linen, and synthetics (nylon, polyester, spandex) can generally be washed. Sometimes silk and cashmere can be hand-washed, and we have seen some silk and cashmere garments with "hand wash" care labels.

Shop Talk MECHANICAL ACTION

Let's take a brief pause from washing machines to talk about one of the most important parts of cleaning that we mentioned briefly: mechanical action, or agitation—a fancy term for rubbing. Remember when we talked about how laundry was done before machines in chapter 1 (page 15), by beating dirty clothes with sticks, rocks at the riverbank, and washboards? To get laundry clean, we need mechanical action to agitate water and detergent through the fibers of the garment. We dry cleaners have special tools and brushes to ensure that our treatments penetrate as much as possible. Without mechanical action, your laundry will not get clean; stains and soil will remain, as will odors. Isn't the whole purpose of doing laundry to remove soil, stains, and odors from our clothes? Before mechanical action can be the hero of the wash cycle, we need to load the machine.

Adding Products and Selecting a Cycle

Now that the machine is loaded, you need to add the detergent, bleach (optional), fabric softener or rinse cycle products (optional), and washing boosters (optional), and select a cycle; but which comes first? In general, we recommend adding the products first and then selecting a cycle. This is to avoid any issues in case you accidentally start the cycle prior to adding products.

A washing machine has compartments to add liquid or powder detergent, and most modern machines have compartments to add bleach and fabric softener. These compartments should be labeled with words and/or symbols to ensure you put the correct product in the proper spot.

Laundry products are dispensed at different times based on their function. For example, laundry detergent is dispensed at the beginning while fabric softener is dispensed last (during the rinse cycle).

Top-of-the-line modern machines sometimes have a special compartment specially designed for laundry detergent pacs; others have reservoirs that auto-dose liquid laundry detergent based on preprogrammed cycles.

1. ADD THE DETERGENT

There are three main types of laundry detergent: liquid, powdered, and predosed products (pacs, tablets, sheets, etc.).

If you are using a predosed product OR powdered detergent, add the product to the tub first and then your laundry. (If you forgot to do this first, try slowly spinning the tub until the product is at the bottom.)

If you are using liquid detergent, you need to add the detergent to the compartment that says "detergent." Read the instructions on the package of the detergent you are using for the amount needed (this is called "dosing"). If your machine does not have a compartment for detergent, add it to the tub before loading your items. Most detergent packaging will give you a guide on how much to use depending on how soiled your

Shop Talk AUTO-DOSING

We are happy to see that some washing machines have the ability to auto-dose liquid laundry detergent and other laundry products as of the early 2000s. Auto-dosing allows the washing machine to dose products based on preset calculations and cycle selection. The machine holds products in reservoirs that need to be refilled every once in a while. This technology is new but has some wonderful advantages and may become a staple of the at-home washing machine. Professional dry-cleaning and laundry equipment have had this capability for decades. It would be nice to see, in the future, residential auto-dosing machines dispense specific types of detergents and additives based on the level of soil, staining, and fabric types.

Shop Talk SUD SENSOR

A sud sensor is a modern addition to washers that serves two functions: 1) most importantly, it turns off the machine if too many suds are detected to ensure that you are not flooded with suds, and 2) it continues rinsing your laundry load until all the suds are gone, because the last thing you want is residual laundry products on your clothing, as this can cause skin irritation for some.

DETERGENT DOSES

LOAD SIZE	LIGHT SOIL	MODERATE SOIL	HEAVY SOIL
SMALL	1 tablespoon	1 tablespoon	2 tablespoons
MEDIUM	1 tablespoon	2 tablespoons	3 tablespoons
LARGE	2 tablespoons	3 tablespoons	4 tablespoons

clothes are and the size of your load. However, we feel that it is not very clear at times, so check out our recommendations above for tips on detergent dosing.

Please, PLEASE, do not add more detergent than what is recommended by us or the bottle—you will keep us up at night! If you properly pretreat stains prior to washing, you will have much better results than if you expect detergent to do the entirety of the stain-removal heavy lifting.

Adding too much detergent actually does more harm than good. The wash cycle is the harshest experience a garment goes through in its life, so the less stressful/aggressive you can make it, the longer your clothes will last. By using too much detergent, you will cause your machine to rinse and repeat (literally) until the sud sensor (see above) gives it the all-clear, adding time and unnecessary steps to your wash process.

We once added way too much detergent to a top-loading machine and had suds (the foam/froth created from the detergent, water, and agitation) overflowing from the top of the machine and onto the floor. It was a mess to clean up.

Long story short, when it comes to detergent, as in most things in life, less is more.

2. ADDING OTHER PRODUCTS (OPTIONAL)

If you are adding fabric softener, liquid bleach, sanitizers, or any other supplemental product, you should add them to the proper compartments now. Some washing machines will have a button to select "softener" or "bleach"; others will automatically take care of this for you if these products are added to the compartment. We are not fans of either liquid fabric softener (page 30) or liquid chlorine bleach (page 29); we do like powdered laundry boosters, such as oxygen bleach (page 29), washing soda (page 29), and borax (page 28). If you are using liquid or powdered laundry detergent, these additional products should be added to the machine's tub before adding your laundry. If you are using a laundry detergent pac, these powders can be added to the powdered detergent compartment.

Before you select your cycle, let's go through a quick checklist:

☐ Is your laundry detergent added?

☐ How about boosters, bleach, and/or fabric softener?

☐ Is your laundry in the machine?

3. CHOOSING A CYCLE

Now that your machine is loaded with laundry and products, you need to turn on the machine and select a cycle. Every washing machine is unique, and you should consult the owner's manual to understand what each cycle means. (You can search online by the manufacturer and model number to find a machine's owner's manual.)

If you are doing laundry in a shared space, such as a laundry room in an apartment building or dorm, check for instructions for the washing machine in the laundry room or on the machine. Here is a general guide about the most common washing machine cycles:

NORMAL OR REGULAR: This is the standard cycle for everyday laundry. It includes washing, rinsing, and spinning to handle a variety of fabrics and soil levels.

HEAVY DUTY: This cycle is designed for heavily soiled or larger loads. It usually involves longer wash times and more vigorous agitation.

DELICATE OR GENTLE: This cycle is for delicate fabrics that require a gentler washing process. It often involves slower agitation and a reduced spin speed to prevent damage to sensitive items.

QUICK OR EXPRESS: This cycle is a shorter version of the normal cycle, intended for lightly soiled items or when you need a quick wash.

PERMANENT PRESS: Designed for wrinkle-resistant and synthetic fabrics, this cycle typically includes a cooldown period at the end to reduce wrinkling.

WHITES: This cycle is optimized for white fabrics and uses hot water to help remove stains and brighten whites.

COLORS: Like the Whites cycle, this cycle uses cold water to prevent color bleeding and fading in colored fabrics.

BULKY OR BEDDING: This cycle is suitable for large and bulky items, like comforters, blankets, and pillows.

HAND WASH: This cycle is designed to mimic handwashing and is suitable for delicate items that require extra care. We do not recommend using this cycle for true handwashing (page 63), as it may damage fragile items. It should not be used to hand-wash wool and cashmere.

RINSE AND SPIN: This cycle is used for rinsing and spinning only, without the washing phase. It's useful for refreshing lightly soiled items or for additional rinsing.

PRESOAK: Some machines have a presoak option that allows you to soak clothes before starting the wash cycle. This can be useful for loosening stubborn stains. This is a good cycle for using oxygen bleach (sodium percarbonate) for brightening or whitening.

SANITIZE: This cycle uses high heat to kill bacteria and allergens, making it suitable for items like towels, underwear, and baby clothes.

At the bare minimum, the washing machine should have options to choose water temperature, cycle time, and, perhaps, a delicate wash. Higher-quality machines may have a crazy number of selections to choose from, such as soil levels and specialty cycles for sanitizing, handwashing, and small pets (that one is not real, but we wanted to see if you are paying attention).

Now, pick the cycle type depending on what you are washing and the water temperature. Most high-quality laundry detergents are formulated to work in cold water. You can save a ton (well, not really a ton but 80 percent) of energy by using cold water rather than hot.

Start Your . . . Washing Machine

After choosing the cycle, press the start button and then wait. Most modern washing machines' cycle times will vary from fifteen minutes to one hour or more. The panel display should show you how much time remains. If your machine has a basic panel with only a timer, expect the normal wash cycle to be thirty to forty-five minutes.

Once the machine starts, it will fill with water and then start agitating, or tumbling, which is called the "wash cycle." This is when the water, detergent, and mechanical action (page 55) clean your clothes, removing stains, soil, and odors. Laundry detergents have ingredients that capture these in the wash water so that they don't end up on your laundry. When soil collects on clean laundry, this is called "redeposition," which is bad; we want soil suspended in the "wash water" to go down the drain.

Shop Talk COLD WATER

Previous generations used to think that white items needed hot water for washing, and dark-colored garments needed cool water; however, that isn't entirely true. Our research has shown that hot water causes fabric shrinkage, fading and color loss, and premature deterioration. Yes, we know we mentioned on page 16 about how in medieval times boiling water was used to wash clothes, but that is not necessary with modern laundry detergents. The only time we think hot water should be used is when you need to sanitize (67) or whiten/brighten your items (page 65); otherwise, cold water is perfectly fine. Again, use a high-quality detergent that is formulated for cold water and your laundry will look beautifully clean.

After the wash cycle, the machine will spin (rotate very, very fast) to remove as much of the wash water (which is where the soil and odors are) as possible. After spinning crazy fast (some as fast as 1,000 to 1,800 revolutions per minute), the tub will stop spinning and more water will be added. This is called the rinse cycle, as you want as much of the detergent removed from your laundry as possible.

Modern washing machine doors SHOULD lock while the machine is spinning, as it is dangerous to your hands (never place your hands into the tub while it is spinning). If your washing machine door can open while the machine is spinning, this means it is broken and should be fixed. However, some older machines and top loaders do not lock the door during the prewash cycle so that you can add products. For example, a good way to whiten whites is by soaking them in powdered oxygen bleach and hot water. Top-loading machines often have a tub soak option so you can do this in the machine.

After the rinse cycle, the machine will spin again to get out as much water as possible, which will help with drying. Once the spin cycle is finished, and the tub has stopped spinning, you can open the door and remove your now-clean laundry from the machine.

Post-wash Inspection

At Jeeves, after every garment is cleaned in the dry-cleaning machines, they are inspected to see if stains remain. If there are still stains, they are treated again. This is a routine you should adhere to as well. In the long run, this extra inspection will save you time and money. Stains that did not come out in the first wash and go through the heat of the dryer may never come out and be "set." This will mean wearing a stained garment or replacing it. If stains remain on a garment after washing, now is the time to put it aside and consult The A-to-Z Stain Removal Guide on page 136.

While machine-cleaning garments is the most common way of doing laundry in the present day, there are a variety of other ways to wash your clothing depending on what's needed. The sections below provide additional information regarding other cleaning methods.

Handwashing

Some garments may have a label that says it can be hand-washed, and some washing machines may have a Hand Wash cycle (page 60). This cycle minimizes agitation and uses cold water. Agitation and hot water are the causes of shrinkage. Most garments that need handwashing will also need to be air-dried.

If your washing machine does not have a Hand Wash cycle, or if you want to control the process yourself, you can hand-wash in a sink or bucket if need be. When it comes to selecting a detergent for handwashing, we have a few recommendations:

- When washing delicate fabrics, like silk or cashmere, use a detergent that is recommended for handwashing.

- For garments that are more resilient than delicates, you can use a regular detergent. For example, a baseball hat can be easily hand-washed with any detergent but would likely be ruined in a machine.

- If you are handwashing all your laundry, we recommend using a laundry detergent soap bar.

You do not need a lot of detergent as you are using a very small amount of water in a sink or bucket compared to a washing machine. We like to use warm water when handwashing, as cold water can be hard on your hands. Here are the steps for handwashing items in a sink:

1. Pretreat any stains and allow the treatment to sit on stains for at least an hour, if possible.

2. Close your sink drain, fill it with warm water, and add the detergent.

3. Mix the detergent into the water. Immerse your items for handwashing and, using your hands, push them down into the water and allow to soak for about 10 minutes or so.

4. After soaking, agitate the garments gently; we use an "up-and-down" motion when handwashing in the Jeeves workroom.

5. For heavily soiled areas, like the headband of a baseball cap, gently rub the area with a soft bristle brush.

6. After agitation, soak your garments for another 5 minutes and then open the sink drain and allow the soapy water to drain. Squeeze (wring) the garments (gently) to remove as much of the soapy water as possible (unless the garment care label indicates "do not wring").

7. Rinse your items to remove the soapy water. (Note: Certain handwashing detergents recommend NOT to rinse after handwashing as they contain additives to keep your items soft, so consult the instructions.) Close the sink drain, fill it with cold water, soak for a few minutes, and then agitate. You may have to repeat this a few times until the rinse water is no longer soapy.

8. After rinsing, squeeze out as much water as possible. We like to start the drying process by laying out a clean bath towel and rolling up the garment in the towel to absorb excess water. After rolling up the towel, allow the garment to dry for 30 to 60 minutes and then remove from the towel and let air-dry. If your garment has a rigid component, such as the brim of a hat or boning, you will not be able to roll it up in a towel, so just lay it flat on a towel and let air-dry.

Soaking

This is our professional method for restoring white garments back to "super white." This technique may also make it possible to remove stains, such as oxidation (yellowing and brown spots caused by stains that dried invisible and now have oxidized from age and heat; see page 96) and other hard-to-remove stains, such as dye transfer.

At Jeeves, in our cleaning department, we use sodium percarbonate, which is an oxygen bleaching agent that does an amazing job of whitening and stain removal. Sodium percarbonate is sold in granular or powder form and needs to be dissolved in hot water. Most brands of oxygen bleach contain sodium percarbonate.

The only downside is that oxygen bleach needs two things to work properly: time (a lot, eight to twelve hours) and hot water (120 to 140°F, or 50 to 60°C). Keep in mind

Shop Talk SODIUM PERCARBONATE

Once dissolved in water, sodium percarbonate (oxygen bleach) becomes hydrogen peroxide, which is a liquid. Hydrogen peroxide is one of our favorite "go-to" stain removers.

that hot water could cause shrinkage, so consult the garment care label to make sure hot water is not an issue.

Just adding a scoop of oxygen bleach during the regular wash cycle is not going to really work. If your washing machine has a Presoak cycle, you can use it; you need to choose the longest time that your machine can be set to presoak. Add about ½ cup (70 g) of oxygen bleach to the tub of the machine before loading the items you want to restore. Add the laundry detergent to your machine, hit start, and then let your machine do its thing.

Our method, which we use in our wet-cleaning department, is to restore items using a bucket rather than the washing machine. This allows us to control the amount of water, and we can soak for as long as we need to get great results. Here are the steps for successful soaking:

1. Add ½ cup (70 g) of oxygen bleach to a bucket and fill it with hot water.

2. With a long spoon or a gloved hand, swish the water to allow the bleach to dissolve.

3. Add the items that you want to restore to the bucket. Using a long spoon or your gloved hand push the items under the water.

4. Allow to soak for 8 to 12 hours.

5. Using gloved hands, remove the items from the bucket and then wash as usual.

6. Pour the water from the bucket down the drain of your sink.

After washing, you should see a noticeable improvement in both whiteness and stain removal.

Sanitizing: Hot Water and Chlorine Bleach

We only recommend the use of hot water when sanitizing garments, re-cleaning heavily soiled garments, or removing mold. The same is true if you are washing dirty cloth diapers or items contaminated with blood, vomit, feces, or urine. Bedbugs, lice, and moth larvae can also be killed by using high-temperature water.

Some washing machines may have a Sanitize cycle (page 61), which heats hot water to over 150°F (65°C) and will kill bacteria and insects. Keep in mind that using super-hot water increases the risk of fabric shrinkage and color fading, and will wear out fibers quicker.

For further sanitizing of your laundry, you can add chlorine bleach. Generally, we do not recommend chlorine bleach for laundry, as it can irritate your skin and eyes and cause irreversible damage to clothing if not used properly. You should use only ¼ cup (60 ml) of chlorine bleach, adding it to the bleach dispenser of your washer, if you want to sanitize your laundry. Chlorine bleach can damage dyes in fabric, so read the instructions carefully on the label.

Pro Tip HOW TO WORK WITH CHLORINE BLEACH

Chlorine bleach can damage the clothes you are wearing if they are splashed with it. We have ruined our own clothes by using a bathroom cleaner with bleach and getting some residual spray on our pants. When working with chlorine bleach, we wear our work clothes (ones we do not care about) and protect our skin with long sleeves and gloves.

When Not to Wash

What shouldn't you wash at home? When we talk about sorting your laundry in chapter 3 (page 33), we suggest that you look at the garment care labels to make sure that everything going into the wash can be washed. Garment care labels, by law in the United States, have to tell the consumer the preferred method of cleaning, not all the methods that can be used.

Other items that you have may be able to be hand-washed rather than machine-washed. And lastly, there are going to be items you own that must be taken to your local dry cleaner.

In the appendix on page 129, you'll find a guide to help you decipher garment care labels, as some are written with symbols rather than words. The red flags you should look out for are:

- Dry clean only
- Do not wash
- Spot clean only
- Leather method only
- Specialty cleaning only

Knowing how to care for your garment should not be difficult, but manufacturers can make reading the garment care label difficult. Even we as professionals can be stumped by labels in garments that just do not make sense. We have seen garments labeled "do not wash," "do not dry clean," "do not iron," and "do not steam." We would have to guess they were made to be worn once or twice, and then . . . ?

Once you "violate" the garment care instructions, you are on your own if the garment gets damaged. Some risks of washing items that the label says not to wash include shrinkage, color bleeding, and change of fabric texture (hand feel).

Shrinkage is the biggest issue because, in most cases, once something shrinks, it cannot be restored. The same is true of color bleeding; if you have a black-and-white garment and the black bleeds into the white, this problem may not be correctable.

With the speed at which fashion moves, it is hard for us to give you complete advice on what you can possibly wash that is labeled "dry clean only." Our suggestion is to proceed with caution. If you have a white cotton top that says, "dry clean only," you can be reasonably certain that this item can be washed. We would start with washing on the Delicate/Gentle cycle with cold water only. Again, there is a risk . . .

Washing Machine Problems and Maintenance

Most major problems, such as leaks or clogged pumps, may require a service call, but you can take care of basic issues yourself. Check the owner's manual for troubleshooting—it is usually in the back of the manual. (If you cannot locate your owner's manual, search online using the make and model number of your washing machine.) Here's how to handle some basic issues:

UNBALANCED LOAD: If your machine is making a racket with loud banging noises, it is not possessed. Typically with top-loading machines, when you are washing towels, the towels may shift to one side of the tub and make a horrible noise when the machine goes into the spin cycle. Press pause and wait for the machine to stop spinning, and then the loading door will unlock. You can then evenly redistribute the load and the problem should be solved. Unbalanced loads could cause your washing machine to "walk" and move around due to this unequal distribution during the spin cycle. This is not an issue with front-loading washers.

ODORS AND SMELLS: Water that does not dry in your washer could lead to mold and mildew growing, which will cause odors. We encourage you to leave the loading door AND product-compartments drawer open so that all areas dry between uses.

LAUNDRY NOT GETTING CLEAN: Using too much, too little, or poor-quality detergents could cause your laundry not to be cleaned well. It is important to use the correct amount of detergent in proportion to the size of the load you are cleaning. See our guide about laundry detergent amounts on page 57 for more information.

ERROR CODES: Sometimes an unbalanced load will cause an error code to display. When we forget to turn the water back on for our home washing machine (we turn off the water supply to our washing machine between uses to prevent a flood if something goes wrong with the machine) and start a cycle, the machine will give us a "no water supply" error code. You may have to consult the owner's manual for the meaning of the code.

WATER LEAKS: It may be as simple as connections at the shut-off valve or into your washing machine that need to be tightened. Most only require hand tightening, but on some, you may need to use a wrench. Don't overtighten, as you could break a fitting. If these hoses are not leaking, you will need to call a mechanic for repair.

Washing machines do not need a lot of routine maintenance, but you can prolong the life of your machine with these tips:

- Follow the manufacturer's instructions for proper usage, load capacity, and detergent amounts.

- Clean the machine regularly, including the tub, detergent dispenser, and filters.

- Run a Tub Clean or Sanitize cycle with a washing machine cleaning tablet in the tub.

- Make sure your washer is secured or stabilized. If it moves around after each load, it needs to have the stabilizing feet adjusted. Not attending to this could cause damage to internal components or misalignment.

- Avoid overloading the machine to prevent strain on the motor and other components.

- Avoid using excessive detergent, as it can lead to buildup and damage.

- Check and maintain the hoses and connections for any leaks or damage.

- Avoid using the machine for items that are not suitable for washing.

- Address any issues or malfunctions promptly by contacting a professional for repairs.

- For front-loading washers, keep the door open between uses to allow the tub to dry; otherwise, odors will build up. Also, the gasket of front-loading machines should be wiped down to remove excess detergent and lint, which could cause leaking.

CHAPTER 6

DRYING BASICS

Check the Garment Care Labels • **74**

Parts of a Dryer • **75**

Loading the Dryer and Selecting a Cycle • **76**

Wrinkle Reduction • **78**

Drying Down, Down-Alternative, and Feather-Filled Items • **79**

Dryer Problems and Maintenance • **79**

Clothesline Drying • **80**

Now that you have washed your clothes, they need to be dried. Clothes dryers most commonly use electricity to generate heat, which dries your clothes, but some also use natural gas or propane. Other methods of drying clothes are clotheslines, drying racks, and drying cabinets.

Check the Garment Care Labels

Check the care label on your clothes to see if anything cannot go in the dryer. Here are the symbols for drying that even for us as professional dry cleaners can be like reading Egyptian hieroglyphs (refer to The Garment Care Label Guide on page 129 for more information on these care labels). The symbols can be tricky to read, but if the label says, "do not tumble dry" or indicates "line dry," "drip dry," dry flat," or any of those variations, do not use your clothes dryer. Colors that may be sensitive to sun exposure may need to be dried in the shade.

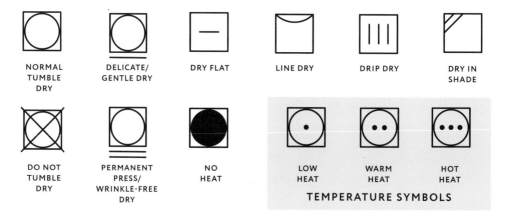

| NORMAL TUMBLE DRY | DELICATE/ GENTLE DRY | DRY FLAT | LINE DRY | DRIP DRY | DRY IN SHADE |

| DO NOT TUMBLE DRY | PERMANENT PRESS/ WRINKLE-FREE DRY | NO HEAT | LOW HEAT | WARM HEAT | HOT HEAT |

TEMPERATURE SYMBOLS

Sometimes these symbols make our heads hurt, as we cannot figure out the difference between "line dry" and "drip dry."

So, if there is anything that you washed that has particularly bad stains or soil, check it before drying it. As we talk about in Post-wash Inspection (page 63), stains can be set, or made impossible to remove, if they go through the heat of a dryer. If stains remain, you will want to treat the stained items again and rewash before drying.

PARTS OF A DRYER

Here are the main components of a dryer that you need to know.

DOOR: A clothes dryer has a door that opens from the front, through which you load your damp laundry into the drum.

DRUM: The drum, also called the basket or wheel, is the part that holds your laundry and spins while your laundry is drying.

CONTROL PANEL: The control panel helps you make your drying cycle selections.

LINT FILTER: This is usually in a slide-out compartment between the drum and the door. The lint filter should be cleaned after every load and checked again before starting the dryer. Not cleaning it will increase drying time, as the airflow in the dryer will be reduced and could be a contributing factor in a dryer fire.

There are a few more parts of the dryer, but we'll get to them later in the Dryer Problems and Maintenance section on page 79.

Pro Tip HOW TO DRY DELICATES

If you washed your delicates in a mesh laundry bag (lingerie bag), remove the items from the bag during drying. Delicate items should be dried on the Low Heat/Delicate cycle, but we prefer to air-dry. If you have anything that you are worried about shrinking, air-dry that item.

Loading the Dryer and Selecting a Cycle

When loading a dryer, do not fill the drum more than halfway full—placing too much laundry in the drum will extend the drying time, and everything will be a wrinkled mess when you remove it.

Now you need to select the dry cycle depending on what types of items you want to dry. Most dryers will have a knob to select among many cycles, though simpler dryers may only allow you to select the level of heat and time. If you can only select a dryer temperature, here are our recommendations, but check the garment care label for the manufacturer's instructions on drying temperatures:

LOW HEAT OR DELICATE: For silk, lace, and garments with elastic, low heat helps prevent shrinkage and damage to fragile fabrics and trim.

MEDIUM HEAT: This is our normal setting, and most clothes are okay with being dried at this setting. Cotton, linen, and synthetic fabrics should be fine at medium heat.

HIGH HEAT: This setting is for towels, bedding, and heavy fabrics, like denim. Keep in mind that high heat will cause more shrinkage, so be careful.

NO HEAT TUMBLE DRY/AIR DRY OR FLUFF: This setting tumbles items without heated air. Super-delicate items, sneakers, and stuffed toys should be dried on this setting.

SANITIZE: Temperatures need to exceed 140°F (60°C) to kill bugs (bedbugs, moth larvae, and lice) and bacteria. At this level of heat, fabrics will wear out sooner and their life will be shortened dramatically.

When we talk about sorting your items for washing in chapter 3 (page 33), we suggest separating light colors from dark colors, as well as by weight and types of fabrics. As we explained on page 38, gym clothes, which are usually made from synthetic materials, are going to be almost dry after coming out of the washing machine, whereas towels and sheets are going to be wetter. So, it is best to dry towels and sheets together and gym clothes and other lightweight items together; otherwise, your gym clothes will be dry long before your towels.

Shop Talk MOISTURE SENSORS

Technologically advanced dryers have moisture sensors that know when your laundry is dry. You will be able to select how dry you want your laundry to be when finished according to the type of items you are drying—and in some cases, you can get a text alert to your phone when your clothes are dry.

FUN FACT

In the United States as of 2009, 80 percent of households own dryers. Some homeowner associations ban clotheslines, considering them unsightly, while in Germany, on the other hand, clotheslines are considered traditional and wholesome. America's love of clothes dryers compared to the rest of the world comes down to cultural differences.

Drying white terry towels with your dark clothes is not a good idea either. Light-colored lint (tiny bits of fiber that separate from fabric during drying) will end up all over your dark clothes, which will be terribly difficult to remove. In extreme cases, rather than spending a lot of time with a lint brush, rewashing the linty clothes is your best bet.

Wrinkle Reduction

Reducing wrinkling at this stage of doing your laundry will save you a ton of time later. Overloading the dryer or mixing towels with T-shirts will be a recipe for wrinkles, so remember to dry "like things together."

Once the dry cycle is completed, first check to make sure that your clothes are dry (if some items are a little damp, that is okay), and then remove everything from the dryer and fold it right away. If you leave your clothes in a heap in the dryer, the residual heat will create wrinkles. We like to give the most wrinkle-prone garments a shake and then lay them flat when unloading the dryer; if you just pull everything out in a heap and then fold, more wrinkling can occur. When storing your clothes after folding them, do not pack them tightly into a drawer or closet. Wrinkles will occur from the weight of the surrounding garments crushing them.

If you do not have time to fold, our method is to remove your clothes from the dryer and lay them flat until you can fold them. We do this with tops and bottoms that tend to wrinkle a lot if not folded right away. You can also remove your clothes from the dryer while slightly damp and allow them to dry on a hanger. Gravity and the weight of the garment will remove some wrinkles.

Drying Down, Down-Alternative, and Feather-Filled Items

When drying anything with down, down alternative, and feather filling, such as winter outerwear and pillows, there is a risk for the down clumping together and not being fluffy. To avoid this, we suggest using the Low Heat setting so that the filling has a lot of time to dry and fluff up. To get rid of the clumps and make your down jacket or pillow fluffy again, you need to put it in the dryer along with something to fluff up the filling—clean dryer balls, new tennis balls, or new sneakers (you don't want to use anything that is soiled when fluffing up the filling) will work. You can also remove the item a few times during the drying process and give it a good shake to help reduce clumping.

Check the label on the item before washing, as not all down and feather products can be washed at home, and some will require the help of a dry cleaner.

Dryer Problems and Maintenance

Clothes dryers do not require much maintenance, but there are things you need to do to keep the dryer running safely. To reduce the risk of a fire from lint buildup and keep your dryer in tip-top shape for a long time, we recommend the following:

- Clean the lint filter after every load and check it again before starting the dryer. If you check it twice, you will never forget. If this filter is clogged with lint, it reduces air flow, which will make drying your clothes take a lot longer than it should. Plus, it increases the risk of a fire.

- Clean and inspect the dryer vent hose and exhaust hood. The vent hose may be plastic or metal and vents the hot dryer air to the exterior of your house. The exhaust hood is where the vent attaches to the outside of your house. Both should be cleaned annually, so you may need to have a professional company inspect and clean these for you depending on how long the vent is. Some dryers used in apartment buildings are "ventless" and have a filter that needs to be cleaned on a regular basis. Consult your owner's manual. (If you cannot locate your owner's manual, you can search online using the make and model number of your dryer.) Excessive lint in dryer vents is the number-one cause of dryer fires.

- The door seal should be cleaned and inspected on a regular basis. If the door seal is worn, cracked, or dirty, you are letting out hot air, which will waste time and energy.

- Clean the drum of the dryer monthly by wiping it down to remove any residue from dryer sheets and fabric softener (if you use these products).

- Do not overload the dryer; this will put a strain on the motor, which could cause premature wear. Overloading can cause overheating and is another cause of a dryer fire.

- If your dryer is making noises, has strange odors, or isn't drying correctly, it's time to call a repair person to check it out.

Clothesline Drying

The benefits of using an outdoor clothesline for drying your laundry are:

- Your laundry will have a clean odor that you cannot get from a clothes dryer.

- Shrinkage should not occur when air-dried.

- There is less wear and tear on your clothes from the heat of the dryer and tumbling.

- No electricity or natural gas is required.

The problem with using a clothesline is that it requires a lot more work and time, cannot be done in the rain, and your neighbors may not want to see your laundry hanging up. A drying rack can be used inside your home to get most of the benefits of a clothesline for items that need to be air-dried. Some racks can be folded up when not in use to save space.

When Jerry was growing up in Corona, in Queens, New York, both his grandmother and mom had clotheslines that went from the second-floor window to a telephone pole. At each end of the clothesline was a pulley. You would hang a garment using clothespins, pull the rope to move the clothesline, and then hang your next item. If it was a windy day and a clothespin fell off a shirt, you would have to see whose backyard the shirt ended up in.

If items feel stiff after air drying, and your dryer has a No Heat Tumble Dry/Air Dry or Fluff cycle, pop those items into the dryer with dryer balls for ten minutes or so. The tumbling with the dryer balls and no heated air will soften them up.

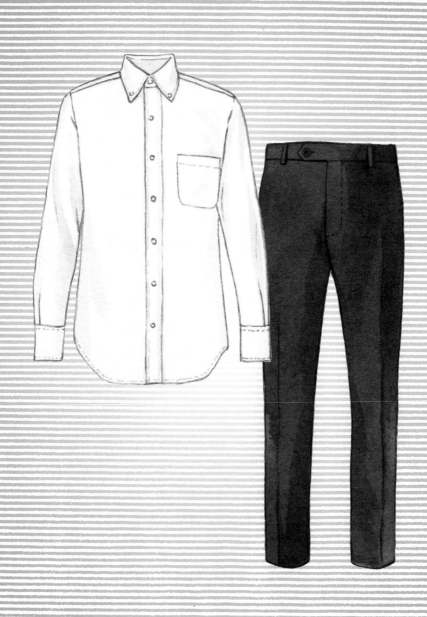

CHAPTER 7

GETTING THE WRINKLES OUT

Steaming • **85**

Ironing • **86**

Hopefully, you have already helped reduce wrinkling while drying your clothes (page 78), but what do you do about items that are still wrinkled and need more love? You can attack this problem in two ways: with a handheld steamer or an iron. In general, steaming relaxes a fabric's fibers and allows wrinkles to soften, while ironing provides a crisp, flat finish, or a solution to stubborn, hard wrinkles. First, steam from the iron softens the wrinkles, and the hot, dry iron removes the residual steam from the fibers and flattens the fibers. This creates a sharp and smooth result.

Here is our list of what fabrics steam well and what you need to use an iron for:

STEAM

- Wool

- Silk

- Knits

- Synthetic

- Acrylic

IRON

- Cotton

- Linen

- Rayon

- Viscose

Steaming

The steamer route is quicker, easier, and usually safer, but will not give you a crisp finish like an iron. Steamers are best used on synthetic fabrics, silk, wool, and sometimes rayon. The best way to steam a garment is to place tops, dresses, jackets, and coats on hangers and bottoms and skirts on clip hangers. Hang the garment for steaming on a clothes rack or shower rod; this will make it easier to work on. Fill your steamer with distilled water, turn it on, and allow it to heat up. Turn on the steam control (be careful not to burn yourself on the hot steam or the area where the steam comes out) and steam should be coming out of the steamer.

Work from top to bottom, using the steamer to release the wrinkles. You may need to hold parts of your garment taut with your free hand to remove stubborn wrinkles. The steam should penetrate through both sides of your garment, though you may need to work on both sides if it's badly wrinkled.

If you do not have a steamer and need to remove wrinkles, you can use your bathroom as a giant steamer. Run your shower on hot to steam up the bathroom. Once it's steamed up, turn off the water. Hang your garments in need of steaming from the shower rod and close the bathroom door. Wait about fifteen minutes and then check to see if the wrinkles were removed. Repeat if necessary. Keep in mind that cotton and linen will not look crisp using this method.

Ironing

Ironing is more complicated than steaming, as you will need an iron and something to iron your clothes on. An ironing board is best, but in a pinch, you can use a bed, or a table covered with a thick towel. The towel will protect the table and your garment, as you should never iron directly on most household surfaces.

Check the instructions for the proper use of your iron. You can start by adding distilled water to the steamer compartment (if your iron has this feature), setting the temperature, and turning it on. There may be a light to indicate when it has reached the correct temperature.

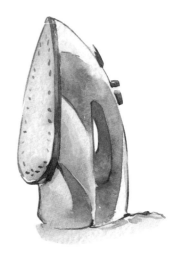

The temperature setting is very important. If you iron a wool garment using the cotton or linen setting, you will scorch and burn the fabric, which isn't good. Some irons have the fabric settings on the temperature dial, whereas others may only have Low, Medium, or High. Here are the recommended ironing settings based on temperature or heat setting:

FABRIC	IRON SETTING	TEMPERATURE (FAHRENHEIT)	TEMPERATURE (CELSIUS)
LINEN	High	445°F	230°C
TRIACETATE	High	390°F	200°C
COTTON	High	400°F	204°C
VISCOSE/RAYON	High	375°F	190°C
WOOL	Medium	300°F	148°C
POLYESTER	Medium	300°F	148°C
SILK	Medium	300°F	148°C
ACETATE	Medium	290°F	143°C
ACRYLIC	Low	275°F	135°C
LYCRA/SPANDEX	Low	275°F	135°C
NYLON	Low	275°F	135°C

CHECK THE GARMENT CARE LABELS

The garment care label will also indicate the correct temperature for ironing. The symbols for ironing and their meanings are below (refer to The Garment Care Label Guide on page 129 for more information on these care labels):

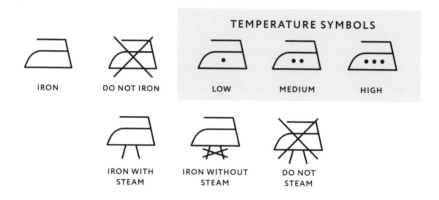

HOW TO IRON

It is best to see visually how to iron rather than follow a written description. We suggest watching videos online for the best tutorials. Nonetheless, here are some basic instructions:

1. Open your ironing board and adjust the height for your comfort. Ironing boards have a pointy end and perhaps a metal area at the other end on which to rest your iron. It will be easier to iron if you orient the ironing board so that the iron's resting end is on your dominant hand's side.

2. Fill the water compartment of the iron with distilled water.

3. Turn on your iron and allow it to come up to the proper temperature. Remember to check the heat setting and choose the proper temperature for the garment you are ironing.

4. Position your garment on your ironing board so that it sits flat; smooth the fabric with your hand. The nose (the rounded or slightly pointy end) of your ironing board is used to iron smaller or hard-to-get-out areas, such as collars, cuffs, and shoulder areas. Some ironing boards have a smaller sleeve board that folds out and is designed specifically for ironing sleeves. If possible, pull your garment across the nose of the ironing board. This will allow you to iron one side at a time, making the task much easier.

5. The most important aspect of ironing is to move the iron in one direction only. If you move "back and forth," you could create creases. Your goal is to iron each section once and to rotate the garment carefully and not wrinkle it too much. Try not to iron multiple layers of your garment at the same time; ideally, you should

Pro Tip HOW TO IRON WOOL

An iron will cause fabric shine on wool fibers if caution is not taken. Wool fibers have loft, which can be crushed by an iron, and, in extreme cases, the fibers can get scorched, creating fabric shine that cannot be restored. Wool items should be pressed using a protective iron cloth placed between the garment and the iron. If you do not have one, turning the item inside out will help minimize possible damage.

Shop Talk SIZING AND STARCH

Both sizing and starch can be
purchased in spray cans either online
or in the laundry section of your
local retail store. Starch, the more
well-known of the two, adds stiffness
to garments and is vegetable-based
(usually made from corn or rice).
Sizing is resinous and can be made
from vegetables or plastic. Sizing adds
body and crispness, makes ironing
easier, and allows fabric to hold pleats
and creases longer. It also prevents
wrinkling while wearing. Starch,
on the other hand, causes fabric to
become overly stiff and wrinkles and
creases to form while wearing. As
professional dry cleaners, we always
recommend to our clients that they
do not starch their garments for
these reasons. Excessive use of starch
will cause your garments to wear out
sooner, as starch causes the fibers to
snap rather than bend when wearing,
causing fraying or, in extreme cases,
holes. The use of starch or sizing is a
personal preference, so we wanted to
tell you about both.

iron one layer of fabric at a time. For cotton and linen, keep a spray bottle filled with distilled water handy. Mist the fabric lightly with distilled water, and you will get a professional finish. Although it has some drawbacks, you can also purchase spray starch or sizing (see opposite) if you want to achieve an even crisper finish on cotton and linen.

6. Once ironed, place your garment on a hanger right away. If you ironed a blouse or shirt, button the top button and a few down the front; this will prevent the fabric from folding and creasing when you hang the top in your closet.

When you are finished using your iron or steamer, drain the excess water; this can prevent or minimize the amount of mineral buildup within the appliance.

CHAPTER 8

HANGING AND STORING YOUR CLOTHES

Hanging Your Garments • **94**

Clean and Mend before Storing • **94**

Out of Space? • **97**

Keeping Clothes Smelling Fresh • **98**

As we have said, the sooner you fold your clothes once they are dry, the fewer wrinkles you will have to deal with. There are online guides and books that show you how to fold just about everything, but we are going to share some of our professional tips and tricks for hanging and storing clothes.

Hanging Your Garments

You don't need to fold garments that you will store on hangers in your closet. The best pro tip and advice we can give you to preserve your clothes for as long as possible is to invest in good hangers. Wire hangers that you may get from your local dry cleaner just won't do. Clothes need to be supported correctly so that they do not get misshapen or damaged by inexpensive wire hangers.

For tops, choose a hanger with a curve to the shoulder so that the end of the hanger doesn't come to a point. Your pants should be folded over a hanger with a padded or nonslip bar. Coats and jackets should be stored on a hanger with a chunky shoulder to preserve the shoulder area.

If you are saving space in your closet, at the least you should use velvet hangers, which are space-saving and a big step up from wire dry-cleaner hangers.

At Jeeves, we return all our clients' knit garments folded to prevent stretching and becoming misshapen. At home, we recommend that knits either be folded over a hanger for closet storage or stored in drawers or on shelves.

Clean and Mend before Storing

Of course, we must address what to do before storing your seasonal clothes. The number-one rule from our professional experience is to "clean and mend before storing." There is nothing worse than taking out a blouse from last season to wear only to find that it is missing a button and you cannot wear it.

If you know how to sew a little and can do minor repairs yourself, amazing! If you do not know how to sew, don't worry; many larger dry cleaners may have a tailor or seamstress who can help you. They can repair open seams and loose linings, take care of missing buttons, and replace broken zippers. Besides repairs, a seamstress or tailor may be able to alter a garment to fit you better.

If your local dry cleaner doesn't have a tailor, search for "tailor or seamstress near me" online. Finding a good seamstress or tailor can help you repair a favorite garment, so it doesn't have to go in the donation bin.

There are lots of reasons to clean your clothes before storing, but here are the top three:

1. Removable stains will set and become permanent.

2. Invisible stains will oxidize (turn yellow/brown) over time.

3. Remaining soil can attract moths.

DON'T LET STAINS SET

Stains will also become more difficult to remove the longer they remain on your garment. Dry cleaners prefer to work on stains that have not had time to "set," which makes them easier to remove. When a stain first occurs, the staining agent (wine, coffee, juice, etc.) sits on top of the fabric. Over time, the stain migrates into the fibers, where it reacts with the dye, fabric, finish, and atmosphere, making it difficult or even impossible to remove.

As part of your laundry routine, you should always treat stains on washable fabrics right away and wash the stained garment as soon as possible. If you get stains on "dry clean only" items, bring it to your local dry cleaner sooner rather than later and let them know what the stain is. We do not recommend attempting to remove stains from "dry clean only" items yourself, but if you did, tell the dry cleaner how you attempted to treat the stain. This will help them remove the stain for you.

STAINS THAT APPEAR AFTER STORAGE

At Jeeves we have dry-cleaned garments that look clean only to have yellow stains appear after cleaning. We have seen this happen with our own laundry at home as well. We call these "invisible stains."

Here is an example of how such a stain might happen: Last August, when you were hanging out and having a glass of white wine or Sprite, you spilled a little on your white top. In the heat of the day, the stain dried and went away; however, the potential problem, those pesky sugar molecules, was invisible and lurking in the background.

White wine and Sprite contain sugars, which, over time, will oxidize and turn yellow. The best way we can explain oxidation is if you take a bite from an apple and then set it on the counter. What happens? The nice, crisp, white interior of the apple turns brown in a short amount of time. This is oxidation, but on a garment, this process takes months, not minutes.

A few months later, when you grab that "what you thought was clean" white top from your closet, you discover that it now has yellow stains. This can also occur when old stains that were not removed in the wash turn yellow or oxidize after being exposed to the heat of the dryer.

ADDRESSING THE ELEPHANT (MOTHS) IN THE ROOM

Did we mention that moths love stains? The best way to prevent moth damage is to put your clothes away clean. What causes moth damage is not the flying moths you see, but the larvae they lay on your woolens. When the larvae hatch, they are hungry, and momma moth isn't around anymore.

So what do they eat? Protein fibers, which is what wool, cashmere, merino, and silk are. Plus, the moth larvae love bits of food, salt from perspiration, and oils from perfumes. They munch away at the stained areas along with the fibers of the knit, creating havoc and holes.

As an extra layer of protection, we suggest that after cleaning your clothes, you should protect them from the ravages of moths by storing them in breathable fabric bags that the moths cannot get into. Never store your clothes in plastic or the plastic bags from the dry cleaner; it is not good for your garments.

We do not recommend the use of mothballs, which are made from naphthalene, or PDB, and release fumes that repel moths and other insect pests. Mothballs are toxic to humans and animals, and make your clothes smell horrible, in our opinion.

As an alternative to mothballs, use sachets filled with cedar shavings or lavender, cedar blocks, or other herbal moth repellents.

Out of Space?

What do you do when you are out of space for your clothes? If you live in an area with seasons, you can rotate your spring/summer clothes with your fall/winter items; otherwise, you can store garments that are seldom worn. We would recommend that if you are out of space, it would be a good time to edit your wardrobe as much as possible and donate items that you are not wearing.

To properly store your clothes, we like to use plastic bins that have tight-fitting lids. This will keep moisture and moths out of your stored clothes. If you have space elsewhere in your home and do not want to use plastic storage bins, we advise against using your attic or basement. Attics can be too hot (even for clothes in plastic bins), and basements are too damp. Dampness can cause musty odors and, in extreme cases, mold growth on your clothes.

VACUUM SEALING

You can purchase large plastic bags to store your clothes, in which you can use your home vacuum to remove all the air in the bag. This compresses your garments, saving space, but in doing so, you may damage your clothes.

Vacuum bags can compress fabrics such as wool, cashmere, silk, and leather, causing permanent wrinkles, cracks, and damage to the fibers. At the very least, when you remove your clothes from the vacuum bag, they will be horribly wrinkled with creases that will take a lot of time and effort to remove—if they come out at all. For these reasons, we do not recommend vacuum bags to store your clothes.

Keeping Clothes Smelling Fresh

Clothes need good air circulation, so as we mentioned earlier, do not store anything (even short term) in plastic bags, including non-breathable garment bags. It is also advisable not to store dirty or malodorous clothes with clean clothes. The smelly clothes will make your clean clothes, well, smelly.

If you have minor odors that you want to remove, you can use your dryer on the No Heat Tumble Dry/Air Dry or Fluff cycle to air them out. If you have a clothesline, fresh air will do wonders to remove odors from your clothes. Lastly, you can purchase clothes refresher sprays, which will also do the trick.

You can store your clothes with sachet bags filled with nicely scented dried flowers, such as lavender or roses. This is a good DIY project, as you can vary what scent your wardrobe has.

CHAPTER 9

WHAT DO DRY CLEANERS DO?

When Should You Go to the Dry Cleaner? • **102**

What the Heck Is Dry Cleaning? • **104**

Wet Cleaning and Stain Removal • **106**

How Dry Cleaners Press and Iron • **107**

How a Dry Cleaner Would Pick a Dry Cleaner • **110**

At this point, your clothes have been cleaned, dried, ironed, and folded. But what do you do when certain items cannot be cared for at home? Well, that's where your friendly neighborhood dry cleaner comes in!

In this chapter, we explain when you should go to a dry cleaner and how their equipment and processes differ from at-home appliances and methods, along with a fun, behind-the-scenes sneak peek of what dry cleaners do.

When Should You Go to the Dry Cleaner?

As third- and fourth-generation dry cleaners, it would be in our best interest to say you should dry-clean everything, but we would not be telling the truth. Dry cleaning is one tool we use to clean clothes, but we use many others as well.

Jerry says: "When I first started working in the family dry-cleaning company, I found a poster from the 1970s used to promote dry cleaning when polyester first hit the market. The big thing about polyester was that it was advertised as 'wash and wear,' meaning it came out of the dryer ready to wear without wrinkles; this was not a good fabric for the dry-cleaning industry. The poster was printed in large letters: 'No matter what the label says, everything dry-cleans better.'"

Maybe in the '70s this was true, but this is not the case now. As professional dry cleaners, we take care of many garments that cannot be dry-cleaned. Our clients rely on us to clean and restore their garments to pre-worn condition, and we at Jeeves use a variety of methods to achieve this. Here's when we recommend that you go to a dry cleaner:

- For any garments labeled "dry clean only."

- If you have a serious stain that you do not think you can remove at home.

- For vintage or antique items that may get damaged in your home laundry.

- For high-value or special items, like a wedding dress.

- For most leather and suede garments.

- For the handling of oversized items, like tablecloths, bed sheets, and upholstery covers.

- If you have issues with dye bleeding or minor shrinkage.

We once had a client come into Jeeves in tears. She had borrowed a dress from her sister without asking and got a small stain on it. The dress was a black-and-white houndstooth check. She searched online and tried to remove the stain with hairspray, which did not remove the stain and left a ring. She then applied water to remove the ring, and the black dye bled into the white. The care label said, "dry clean only," because of the potential of the black dye bleeding into the white. With a lot of work and skill, we were able to fix the issue, removing the original stain and correcting the dye bleeding. She was eternally grateful, and we do know her sister never found out about the disaster that we averted!

Dry cleaners can be a huge help with problematic garments, so look for a great one (page 110).

What the Heck Is Dry Cleaning?

First, you should know that there is a difference between a dry cleaner and dry cleaning. A dry cleaner uses a variety of cleaning solvents, water included, and processes to clean clothing. Dry cleaning is the specific act of using waterless solvents to machine-clean clothing. For example, dry cleaners excel at servicing men's button-down shirts. But these shirts are usually wet-cleaned and rarely dry-cleaned, as they are cleaned more effectively in water. The main benefit of having a dry cleaner service a shirt like this is the quality of the ironing it will receive from special pressing equipment. More on this equipment on page 107 and back to dry cleaning!

Dry cleaning is similar to how you wash your clothes at home. Instead of water, we use dry-cleaning solutions (solvents) that are liquids but do not contain water. But wait a second, if dry cleaning uses a liquid, then why is it called "dry cleaning"? Well, the chemical definition of a liquid solvent that does not include water is DRY, while liquid solvents that include water are WET. This is why the process is called "dry cleaning," because it contains no water. Confused? Don't get mad at us, take it up with the next chemist you run into.

FUN FACT

The invention of dry cleaning happened in 1821 by Thomas Jennings, who was the first African American to be granted a US Patent, for his chemical cleaning method that he called "dry scouring." In France in 1845, Jean Baptiste Jolly opened a dry-cleaning business in Paris, cleaning clothes in a mixture of gasoline and kerosene.

So what types of solvents do modern dry-cleaning machines use? Most are derived from petrochemicals, liquid silicone, or alcohol, which are referred to as solvents.

Now that you have a vague understanding of the dry-cleaning process, let's talk about machines. A dry-cleaning machine resembles a giant front-loading washing machine. When your clothes are dry-cleaned, they go through a similar process to home laundry. Here is our procedure at Jeeves for every garment:

1. Every garment care label is read.

2. Garments that may be a problem are tested for dye and fabric stability.

3. All stains are pretreated.

4. Loads are sorted by fabric type, color, and weight.

Once the dry-cleaning machine is loaded, we select the cycle depending on what we are cleaning, much like a washing machine. The garments in the dry-cleaning machine go through the following cycles:

1. Wash, using dry-cleaning solution (remember, no water is used) and detergents.

2. Rinse, with clear dry-cleaning solution, sizing, or optical brighteners added.

3. Extraction (high-speed spin).

4. Drying, to evaporate and remove all dry-cleaning solution from your clothes.

Modern dry-cleaning machines ensure that all dry-cleaning solutions are removed from every garment during the drying process. The drying cycle continues until sensors detect that the level is below the legal limits. Unlike home laundry, dry-cleaning solutions are reused, as they cannot be released into the wastewater stream. Dry-cleaning machines have sophisticated filtration and distillation systems so that after each use, the dry-cleaning solution has been perfectly cleaned and sanitized for the next load of cleaning.

The entire dry-cleaning process can take from an hour to an hour and a half, depending on what is being cleaned. Just like with home drying, some garments dry quicker than others.

Wet Cleaning and Stain Removal

What you may not know about dry cleaning is that it does a horrible job of removing most common stains. Dry cleaning excels at removing oil-based stains like makeup and grease, but most stains we get on our clothes are water-based: sweat, blood, coffee, wine, grass, and ink, among others. This means these common stains need water for removal, which dry cleaning does not contain. So what do we do? Use water!

Dry cleaners also use sophisticated water-based, or wet-cleaning machines. These machines look very similar to at-home front-loading washing machines but have a few key differences. The first is how products such as detergents and conditioners are added. Instead of manually dosing and adding products before every cycle, they operate like a soda fountain. The cleaning products are dispensed into each machine through a system of tubes depending on what the selected cycle calls for. This dosing system is gaining traction within the residential washing-machine market. Second, there are usually many more cycles  to choose from compared to an at-home machine. Plus, the operator can usually build a custom cycle if the preset selections are not to their satisfaction. The last key difference is a bit more obvious, as these machines are usually much larger than at-home units. You may be thinking, There must be more to cleaning clothes professionally than just wet cleaning or dry cleaning . . . ? And you'd be right! Just about anyone can operate these machines; the real art is removing stubborn stains by hand.

At Jeeves, garments with stains go through an extensive process of stain removal both prior to and after dry cleaning. The dry-cleaning techs at Jeeves (shout-out to Abby and Mel!) have decades of experience with the art and science of stain removal. The experts who handle the actual cleaning within a dry cleaner are known as spotters.

To remove stains, the spotter needs to have a knowledge of fibers, fabrics, dyes, garment construction, and chemistry. Spotters treat individual stains with a variety of stain-removing agents, which include acids, alkalies, surfactants, oxygen bleaches, and dye strippers. If you looked at their stain-removal workstation, or spotting board, you would see about twenty-one stain-removal products being used along with a steam/air/water gun and vacuum system.

Complicated stains may take hours to remove successfully, and it is easy to go too far with stain removal and cause damage to the surrounding dye of fibers. Great dry cleaners are experts at stain removal.

How Dry Cleaners Press and Iron

Now that all the items are stain-free and thoroughly cleaned, the dry cleaner needs to press and iron them. Unlike in the cleaning department, there are very few similarities between at-home pressing equipment and professional equipment. Here is a brief overview of how dry cleaners remove wrinkles and ensure your garments look as good as possible.

Dry cleaners use large pressing machines that are specialized depending on the items being ironed. The most common professional pressing machine looks like a clam shell made of two ironing boards attached with a hinge. These "boards" are covered in fabric and allow steam to pass through their entire length. This allows the operator to steam and iron a large amount of the garment in a short amount of time.

Most pressing stations have a hand iron off to the side for touch-ups. The steam that drives these units comes from large oil- or gas-fired boilers that generate about 30 psi (psi = pounds per square inch, or a measure of pressure) of pressurized steam (135°F, or 57°C).

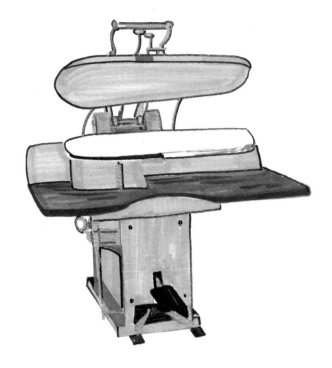

Professional pressing equipment may require the operator to bring the head down manually using muscle power (arms and feet) or controlled with two buttons using air pressure. The press has a release button to open the head, a hand-operated steam valve to release steam from the head, a foot-operated steam valve for steam from the buck, and a foot-operated valve to vacuum the buck.

Why vacuum? The way pressing works is that steam hydrates the fibers, allowing them to expand to release wrinkles, but to get a crisp finish, you need to remove the moisture. The heat from the head will dry the fabric when "ironing," but to speed up the process, a vacuum attached to the buck helps enormously.

At the core, every dry cleaner will most likely have a Hoffman manual press (see illustration above) or similar. This type of press does a good job of pressing most garments, but there are other presses that do a better job on specific types of clothes or household items, such as sheets.

Dry cleaners use different types of presses so that they can give their clients better results than they can achieve at home; plus, professional pressing equipment saves time (labor).

Some of the specialized pressing equipment you may find at a dry cleaner include:

HOT HEAD (NO FABRIC ON THE METAL PLATE ON THE HEAD) PRESSES: These are used for cotton/linen items. Jeeves has a nine-foot-long (2.7 m) hot head press that we use for ironing sheets and tablecloths.

ROLLER PRESSES: These are used for sheets and tablecloths that are too long for a regular press. We feed in the sheet and a roller drum does the pressing. Some models fold the sheet when it exits the press.

FORM AIR FINISHER: This sends steam and then hot air through a form to help with the final pressing. Some are designed for tops, jackets, and coats; others are for pants.

PANT PRESSER: This presses both pant legs at once, giving a perfect crease.

SHIRT UNITS: This is a hybrid of a hot head and a form air finisher, which enables mass pressing of men's shirts. A rotating unit with two operators can press up to seventy-five shirts per hour, with reasonable pressing quality. This unit is paired with a machine that presses the collar and cuffs of each shirt.

Pro Tip DON'T RUSH

If you have a garment that is badly stained, embellished, vintage, or needs special care, do not ask for RUSH service. Give the dry-cleaning company enough time to work on your garment without rushing the service. Some stains and highly embellished garments take a lot of time to clean to get great results.

SWEATER BOARD: This is a steam and vacuum–only press, without a head. It enables the operator to lay out sweaters and knits for blocking, and foot pedals offer steam and vacuum only.

Don't worry; we didn't forget about the most important tool: the hand iron. Surprisingly, the irons we use are similar to residential ones; however, instead of having a water reservoir and electric cord, they are fed steam directly from the dry cleaner's boiler.

The item is now reaching the end of its tour within the dry cleaner. Other equipment worth noting are the automated packaging equipment and distribution conveyors (a fancy term for the big machine that spins and dispenses your clothes when you pick them up from the dry cleaner).

How a Dry Cleaner Would Pick a Dry Cleaner

In the past, we would have recommended looking for a dry cleaner that does the "work on premise," but as environmental regulations have changed over the years, many dry cleaners do their dry cleaning off-site, in commercial rather than residential areas.

Going to the closest dry cleaner to where you live may not be the best option, as anyone can open a dry-cleaning company. As we mentioned earlier, the art of dry cleaning is in the safe removal of stains and ensuring that your garment does not get damaged during the cleaning process. You can check online reviews to find a good dry cleaner, or contact a local boutique and ask if they have a recommendation.

A good dry cleaner's shop should be clean and well organized. We have seen too many dry cleaners that are dirty and have clothes hanging everywhere. This is not a good start. The front counter staff of the dry cleaner should be knowledgeable about the likelihood of stain removal and the dry-cleaning process.

When you drop off your clothes, you should receive an itemized receipt listing all the items you dropped off. The counter staff should ask about stains—please tell them honestly what the stain is and how long it has been there. Trust us, we have heard it all and nothing is embarrassing to a professional dry cleaner. Plus, it helps us remove the stains from your clothes. For example, if a stain is a year old, tell us.

The dry cleaner you choose should be using a computer system to track your clothes; we would shy away from those who are still hand-writing receipts. At Jeeves, we photograph every item that we receive from our clients, so we have both a written and visual record of what they gave us.

The reputation of the dry cleaner is the most important aspect of choosing a great one. A dry cleaner should stand behind all the work they do, have full-value insurance for everything in their care, and be willing to give you advice.

If your dry cleaner has returned your garment with a stain that was not removed, they should have noted why the stain was not removed. We recommend having an honest discussion about the next steps with your dry cleaner to sort out how to proceed; they SHOULD re-clean your garment at no additional cost. Sometimes removing a stain or the last traces of a stain could damage the surrounding dye or fabric. At Jeeves, if we are unable to completely remove a stain, we attach a Quality Report, which lets our client know that we are willing to try further stain removal (at no additional cost) and informs them of the risks associated with it. If they would like us to continue the stain-removal process, they would be informed of the risks and should not hold us responsible if the garment is then damaged.

At times, we will test a badly stained garment, and if we feel we cannot improve it, we will return the garment to our client without charge. We feel this is good business and shows a high level of responsibility. We need to sleep at night and do not want to take our client's money if we cannot improve the wearability of their garment.

If you cannot find a great dry cleaner near where you live, some luxury dry cleaners, such as Jeeves, offer shipping. We have clients from all over the United States who send us garments for cleaning, and we ship them back in specially designed wardrobe boxes.

CHAPTER 10

THE LAUNDRY CYCLE, RINSE AND REPEAT

How Often Should You Wash Your Stuff? • **114**

Laundry Hacks to Make Doing Laundry Fun • **118**

Zach and Jerry's Laundry Routine • **119**

Setting up a routine for laundry will make this task less daunting and stressful (if you find doing laundry stressful). We have found that not waiting too long between "laundry days" is the best way to manage this task. Once the laundry baskets are overflowing, then something enjoyable may become less of a joy and more of a chore. Personally, we have found that doing laundry more frequently makes it easier for us—if you're able to, doing laundry about twice a week will also help prevent stains and odors setting on your items.

If you are fortunate and have a washer and dryer in your home, you can take care of laundry anytime. We find that starting laundry first thing in the morning suits our schedules and mindsets, as we are early risers. If you are a night person, starting laundry after dinner may work best for you.

For those who use a shared laundry room or laundromat, you will need to be more strategic, as there is a lot of waiting around when doing laundry. If the laundry room is in the same building as your home, you can build a schedule around the amount of time it takes between cycles and using the laundry room during off-peak hours.

In one apartment building Jerry lived in, he would start the wash cycle (which was forty-six minutes long) and head to the gym next door. He then would take a break from working out, hang up all the items he wanted to air-dry, and transfer the washed items into the dryer. Since the dry cycle was fifty minutes, he could work out a bit more, take a shower, and then fold the dry clothes. Jerry was able to use his time efficiently. You can figure out what works best for you, as this is just one idea that worked for him.

How Often Should You Wash Your Stuff?

Here is a question we get asked all the time: Do you need to wash your clothes and other items every time you wear or use them?

Well, for items that pick up body odors quickly, such as undergarments, socks, tights, and workout clothes, these should be washed after every wear. Any garment that you have perspired in should be washed after wearing it. The chemical makeup of perspiration, in some cases, could cause discoloration in the underarm areas if left unwashed for too long. These garments may also smell if not washed.

Anything that has gotten stained should be pretreated (see chapter 4 on page 41) and washed as soon as possible. As professional dry cleaners, we have learned that the more time that transpires between when a stain happens to when it is treated, the more difficult it becomes to remove it. So treat stains quickly.

Here is how frequently we recommend washing your items (in alphabetical order):

ATHLETIC WEAR: After every wear.

BABY ITEMS: After every use.

BATH TOWELS: At least once a week, or after three or four uses. Gym towels and washcloths should be washed after every use, as they tend to pick up perspiration and body odors.

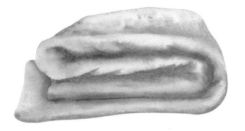

BLANKETS (WASHABLE): At least monthly.

COMFORTERS: At least every three months if used with a duvet cover; otherwise, wash once a month. They can be difficult to wash at home, depending on how large and heavy they are. Check the label for washing instructions, as we have seen some that, unbelievably, cannot be washed and need to be spot-cleaned or dry-cleaned.

DRESSES (CASUAL/WORK): After every few wears.

DRESSES (COCKTAIL): After every wear.

DRESSES (EVENING/BALL GOWN): After every wear.

DRESSES (WEDDING): Hopefully only once in your life! We recommend getting your dress professionally pressed before the big day and washed and preserved after to avoid yellowing/oxidization of the fabric.

DUVET COVERS: At least once a week if you do not use a top sheet, but they can be washed less frequently if you use a top sheet and are not in direct contact with the duvet. We are big fans of duvet covers, as they keep the comforter that goes inside clean for a long time.

KITCHEN TOWELS, NAPKINS, AND TABLECLOTHS: After every use. Food, wine, and oil stains should be pretreated and washed as soon as possible. Kitchen towels should only be used once to make sure bacteria does not build up, especially if they were used to clean up messes.

OUTERWEAR: Once a year.

PAJAMAS: After three wears.

PANTS (WORK): As needed, or after every few wears for those working in an occupation that causes lots of soiling.

PANTS/SLACKS (CASUAL, DRESS, AND SUIT): At least once a month if worn frequently. Hanging up creased pants should prevent you from having to bring them to a dry cleaner frequently.

PILLOWS: At least twice a year for good hygiene and to keep them lasting longer. Some pillows come with pillow protectors, which can be zipped off and washed. We have outlined special washing instructions for pillows on page 195.

SHEETS AND PILLOWCASES: A minimum of once per week (washed or swapped out). Sheets accumulate dead skin, oils, bodily fluids, hair (human and pet if you have one), dust, dust mites, and other gross stuff. Plus, we spend hours and hours in bed. If you have a skin condition, such as eczema or allergies, we recommend washing your sheets more frequently to remove potential allergens.

SUITS: Every few months.

SWEATERS: Every few months and before you put them away for the season.

SWIMWEAR: Rinse after every use and wash every few uses.

TOPS: After every few wears if not stained or perspired in. This really depends on you; if you like to wear clothes that are pressed and freshly cleaned, you may want to wash these items every time you wear them.

TUXEDOS: After every wear.

UNDERGARMENTS: After every wear, though thermal wear and bras may be stretched to after a few wears. This category includes garments such as underwear, bras, tank tops, undershirts, thermal undergarments, and socks.

These recommendations are guidelines only, and if you have pets, children, perspire heavily, or eat in bed, you probably will want to wash more frequently depending on your situation.

Laundry Hacks to Make Doing Laundry Fun

Our best advice to you is to be as organized as possible with your laundry tools. Having everything you need when you need it will make doing laundry easier, and you will get better results. The goal of this book is for you to get great results with your laundry the first time. It's no fun to have to rewash items because stains or odors did not come out.

A DIY stain remover we commonly use is dish soap (Dawn) mixed with water. We recommend storing this mixture in an opaque plastic squirt bottle with a flip top for easy application for stain pretreatments (an opaque bottle prevents UV rays from penetrating the mixture and making it less effective). You can label it with blue masking tape and a Sharpie—no need for a label maker. This is how we keep track of the stain removers we use at Jeeves in our dry-cleaning and laundry departments, though we have at least fifteen different ones that we use daily.

You can also purchase a cleaning caddy to keep all your stain removers, oxygen bleaches, brushes, and other products and tools in one place, making your life so much easier. We use cleaning caddies when we take care of in-home cleaning for drapery and upholstery for our clients. So, these hacks are what the pros use!

We find that listening to music, podcasts, or audiobooks is a great way to pass the time when doing laundry. As we mentioned earlier, we have also worked out at the gym while doing our laundry.

The best hacks we can give are to follow our sorting guide, invest in a laundry sorter, pretreat stains, use high-quality detergent, know when to use oxygen bleaches, dry everything so wrinkles are not a problem, and fold your stuff as soon as it comes out of the dryer.

When we come to think of it, this whole book is a "hack" to make laundry less of a chore. Again, we want you to do it right the first time.

Zach and Jerry's Laundry Routine

You may be wondering, How do the authors do their laundry? Well, here you go! This is our laundry routine:

1. We like to sort our items thoroughly, first by color and then by weight. This is mostly to avoid over-drying of certain fabrics. There's nothing worse than heavily wrinkled gym clothes or cracked graphics on favorite T-shirts due to over-drying.

2. One of our favorite tips is to keep your favorite all-purpose stain-removing spray hanging on the side of your hamper. This way you can sort and pretreat stains the day they occur, which will greatly improve the odds of stain removal. Plus, you don't have to worry about remembering to do it on laundry day!

3. In general, we wash all our clothing in cold water. Please remember that most of your clothing isn't very dirty. The vast majority of soil on your clothing, by weight, is sweat and body oil, not food stains. Water and a high-quality detergent will sort this out for you. Our favorite additives are ¼ cup (30 g) of washing boosters (we like to use a mixture of two-parts washing soda and one-part each of baking soda, borax, and sodium percarbonate).

4. When we have an especially soiled garment, we make sure to inspect it before drying. If the stain is still present, we repeat the stain-removal process, allow the pretreatment to sit on the stain for a bit longer, and then increase the water temperature incrementally during re-washes.

5. As for drying, we prefer to hang-dry all athletic wear, as synthetic fabrics like polyester and elastic don't take long to dry and break down much faster when tumble-dried. Natural fibers like cotton do well in the dryer with low to medium heat. Another of our favorite tips is to stop the drying cycle a few minutes before it's done, when the garments are ever so slightly damp; this will help avoid wrinkles and hard creases.

CHAPTER 11

THE JOY OF CLEAN CLOTHES

Laundry and Our Mental State • **122**

Laundry, Health, and the Environment • **123**

Laundry and Intimacy • **124**

Putting on a soft cotton sweater that is still warm from the clothes dryer, feeling the warmth on your body, along with the scent of clean, fresh cotton, or slipping into your bed, freshly made, with crisp percale sheets, how does this make you feel? For us, these are moments that make us smile.

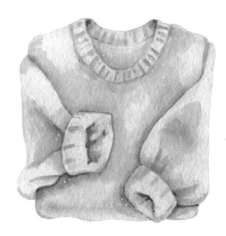

The simple act of wearing a clean garment, using a towel that is still warm from the dryer, or lying down on clean sheets can trigger sensory pleasures that can be enjoyable and soothing. We also find happiness in the scent of clean laundry. For us, it is calming and reminds us of childhood.

Clean laundry can inspire us to appreciate the simple pleasures in life. It's a reminder that even in the ordinary and the everyday, there can be moments of joy and contentment.

Laundry and Our Mental State

The smell of clean laundry is a trigger for some people and gives them happiness and joy. Whether the trigger is the smell of clean cotton or the fragrance of the laundry detergent, nonetheless, the fragrance can evoke a pleasant memory.

Doing laundry embraces being in the moment, allowing you to forget the past. If folding or ironing is a task that you do not enjoy, finding accomplishment with completing the task, as well as decluttering or organizing, may help your sense of well-being.

Clean clothes improve your appearance, which can instill confidence and boost your mood. Wearing clean clothes has even been proven to improve mood. A study done by P&G found an association between mood and the cleanliness of clothes. Furthermore, ongoing research suggests that wearing clean clothes may offer cognitive benefits, such as improving creativity.

There was also a study done that found that folding laundry lowered levels of cortisol, a stress hormone, in people compared to those who did a non-laundry task. Folding or ironing clothes can have a calming effect on some people, like meditation; for others, it may seem like a chore.

Clean clothing is also a symbol of care, which shows attention to detail and pride in your appearance and well-being. Having a clean and organized wardrobe reduces stress, as you will be able to wear your favorite outfit and not have to dig it out from a pile of dirty laundry.

Laundry, Health, and the Environment

Practically, clean laundry is healthier and better for you. Washing removes foul odors, bacteria, germs, mites, and soil. In extreme cases, clean clothes can help reduce infectious diseases, respiratory infections, and skin infections. Clothes pick up bacteria and fungi, and our warm, moist bodies make an ideal environment for these to grow.

Cleaning your clothes also helps them last longer, as mites and soil are abrasives that wear down the fibers of your clothes if you do not wash them regularly. Keeping your clothes longer has an environmental impact because you are not discarding clothes destined for the landfill.

One of the biggest changes you can make to help our planet is to switch from warm or hot water to cold. By making this switch, you can reduce the amount of energy used during the wash cycle by about 80 percent. Using cold water, especially with modern machines and detergents, will also help your clothing last longer by making the wash environment much less harsh.

Laundry and Intimacy

Clean sheets also promote better sleep and intimacy. A study in 2021 by the National Sleep Foundation found that 73 percent of people sleep better on fresh sheets. The fresh scent of clean sheets can also contribute to a restful sleep.

In the intimacy department, over 50 percent of people felt that clean sheets put them in a better mood. In a study of one thousand women in Britain, 52 percent said that dirty sheets were the biggest turnoff and mood killer, while 65 percent of women in the same study said they were more likely to be intimate with their partner in clean sheets.

And to answer that burning question: Should you wash your sheets after being intimate? Bodily fluids, saliva, and sweat can cause bacterial growth that our skin should not contact. These human biohazards, which can end up on the sheets, can cause dermatological woes like body acne. Either protect your sheets with another layer of fabric during intimacy or wash your sheets the day after.

YOUR
LAUNDRY
JOURNEY

W e hope that this book helps you and provides a resource for the future; it is our intention to provide you with information that is somewhat timeless. As we said at the beginning of this book, we want to give you the skills to do your laundry right the first time.

Consult our website, The Clean Club (thecleanclub.com), for information on laundry products, how-to videos, and updates. We can also be found @Jeeves_ny on social media, where we can continue to teach you new laundry skills that will save you time and effort. Here are some parting tips:

- To stay ahead of laundry, we like to do certain loads on a schedule. By having a schedule you can plan and choose which day you change your bed linens and wash them on that day along with bath towels. As you are washing those items, you can pretreat stains on your regular garments and schedule to take care of the following day. But by all means, this is only a suggestion.

- As you are folding your laundry, sort it so that it can be put away easily. This is a huge time-saver that not many people follow. There is nothing worse than having to look through your folded laundry for your favorite jeans, only to then have to refold a bunch of stuff.

- It is nice to fold your clothes on a counter or high table so as not to strain your back; your comfort should always come first. Having a nice place to take care of your laundry will also make the task less daunting. If you can make your laundry room nice, do so.

- Find humor in the task of doing laundry by listening to comedy podcasts or watching comedy videos. Laughter is contagious and may make doing laundry more enjoyable.

- Ask someone else in your household to help with the task. For example, some people don't mind sorting and washing but hate to fold. Maybe you live with someone who likes to fold and iron? Two or more people taking care of laundry will cut down on the time spent by everyone.

- If you are getting overwhelmed by your laundry, break up the task into smaller pieces. Try not to do too much all at once.

- Change your mindset about laundry. Don't think of it as a chore; instead, consider it a way to take care of yourself and your living space. Find joy in the sense of accomplishment.

- Lastly, reward yourself somehow for finishing the task of doing laundry.

You should also reward yourself for finishing this book. We hope you found it informative, entertaining, and helpful and are thankful that you have a copy!

APPENDICES

The Garment Care Label Guide • **129**

The A-to-Z Stain Removal Guide • **136**

How to Care for Different Fabrics •**196**

How to Care for Special Items • **200**

THE GARMENT CARE LABEL GUIDE

The care label must include these important pieces of information:

- The brand name and where the product was made.

- Fabric composition in decreasing percentage order.

- Permanent attachment so that it is easily accessible to the consumer at the point of purchase. Generally, it is placed on the side or bottom of a garment.

- How to care for the item, which, in our opinion, is the most important piece of information,

There are five care-labeling systems: International, Japanese, Canadian, European, and American. Each system has different, albeit similar, requirements for information that must be shown. We will only be covering the American care system; however, most are similar to one other.

This guide includes an illustration of the care symbol, the main description, and a sentence or two for guidance.

Washing Symbols

The washing symbols denote the recommended cleaning process and temperature for an item.

 MACHINE WASH: This symbol is shown as the profile of a top-loading washing machine or just a circle. It usually includes a dot(s) inside that signifies the recommended water temperature.

 PERMANENT PRESS/WRINKLE-FREE WASH: This symbol has a single line below the Machine Wash symbol and is usually for synthetic items. This wash cycle is typically shorter than the normal cycle and uses lower water temperatures.

 DELICATE/GENTLE WASH: This symbol has two lines below the Machine Wash symbol and is usually for fragile items. This cycle is typically very gentle and uses the coolest water temperature.

 HAND WASH: This symbol has a hand with the Machine Wash symbol and is for garments that should be handled with extreme care. While many modern washers have a Hand Wash cycle, we recommend proceeding with caution and washing the item by hand (see Handwashing on page 63).

 DO NOT WASH: This symbol has an X through the Machine Wash symbol. Simply put, do not wash. The item will likely be damaged if washed with water.

 WRING: This symbol looks like a twisted piece of cloth and means the item can be wrung out after washing.

 DO NOT WRING: This symbol has an X through the Wring symbol. The item cannot be wrung after washing. The stress from wringing will likely cause damage to the item.

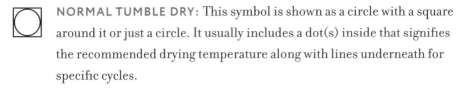

TEMPERATURE SYMBOLS: The most common temperature symbols have one, two, or three dots; however, four and five dots are sometimes shown. One dot is for cold water (86°F, or 30°C), two is for warm water (104°F, or 40°C), and three is for hot water (125°F, or 50°C). These dots denote similar ascending temperatures in the drying and ironing symbol but do not equate to the same temperatures. Most high-quality detergents are formulated to work well in cold/cool water temperatures, and our advice is to wash on cool/cold when possible. Using hot water should be reserved for sanitizing clothing and removing stubborn stains. Frequent use of hot water will cause your clothing to fall apart sooner and lose their color.

Drying Symbols

The drying symbols denote the recommended drying and heat instructions for an item. We believe these are the most challenging symbols to understand, as they have the most unique number of symbols due to the variety of ways to dry things.

NORMAL TUMBLE DRY: This symbol is shown as a circle with a square around it or just a circle. It usually includes a dot(s) inside that signifies the recommended drying temperature along with lines underneath for specific cycles.

PERMANENT PRESS/WRINKLE-FREE DRY: This symbol has a single line below the Normal Tumble Dry symbol and is usually for synthetic items. This drying cycle is typically shorter than the Normal cycle and uses lower temperatures.

DELICATE/GENTLE DRY: This symbol has two lines below the Normal Tumble Dry symbol and is usually for fragile items. This cycle is typically very short and uses the lowest temperature.

NO HEAT: This symbol is the Normal Tumble Dry symbol filled in with black. The item should be tumbled in a dryer without heat, which is often known as the No Heat Tumble Dry/Air Dry or Fluff cycle.

DO NOT TUMBLE DRY: This symbol has an X through the Normal Tumble Dry symbol. The item will likely be damaged if dried in a tumble dryer.

TEMPERATURE SYMBOLS: The most common temperature symbols have one, two, or three dots; however, four and five dots are sometimes shown. One dot is for low heat (125°F, or 50°C), two is for warm heat (135°F, or 55°C), and three is for hot heat (140°F, or 50°C). These dots denote similar ascending temperatures in the washing and ironing symbols but do not equate to the same temperatures.

LINE DRY: This symbol has a square with a wide U shape at the top, like an envelope. The item should not be put in a tumble dryer but air-dried on a clothesline. We believe that this symbol recommends the same drying process as Drip Dry.

DRIP DRY: This symbol has a square with three vertical lines inside it. The item should not be put in a tumble dryer but air-dried on a hanger. We recommend that you hang the wet garment above a sink or in a bathtub or shower. We believe that this symbol recommends the same drying process as Line Dry.

DRY IN SHADE: This symbol has a square with two diagonal lines in the upper-left corner. The item should be line or drip dried but not exposed to sunlight. This is likely because the item's fabric could be damaged by UV rays.

DRY FLAT: This symbol has a square with a single horizontal line inside it. The item should be laid flat on a towel and air-dried. This is likely because the item may be damaged if tumble- or line-dried. In our experience, this method of drying is common for knits and sweaters that would be stretched if dried on a hanger.

 DO NOT DRY: This symbol has a square with an X through it. Honestly, we have no idea what this one means. How can an item be washed and then not dried? If you figure out what "do not dry" means, we'll give you an award.

Bleaching Symbols

The bleaching symbols denote the recommended bleaching instructions.

 ANY BLEACH: This symbol has a triangle and means any type of bleach (chlorine or oxygen bleach) can be used on the item.

 NON-CHLORINE BLEACH: This symbol has a triangle with two diagonal lines inside it and means not to use chlorine bleach on the item; only oxygen bleach, such as hydrogen peroxide or sodium percarbonate (the main active ingredient in most powdered oxygen bleaches), can be used on it. Oxygen bleach is also known as color-safe bleach.

DO NOT BLEACH: This symbol has a triangle with an X through it and means not to use any type of bleach on the item.

Ironing Symbols

The ironing symbols denote the recommended ironing process and temperature for an item.

 IRON: This symbol has the shape of an iron. It usually includes a dot(s) inside that signifies the recommended ironing temperature.

 DO NOT IRON: This symbol has the iron shape with an X through it and means that the item cannot be ironed.

 STEAM: This symbol has the iron shape with two short, angled "steam" lines coming out of its base and means that the item can be steamed.

 DO NOT STEAM: This is the Steam symbol with an X through it and means that the item cannot be steamed.

 DO NOT IRON WITH STEAM: This symbol often has two iterations: An X only through the steam lines at the bottom or an X through the entire iron and steaming symbol. Only use the heat of the iron; do not press the steam button. We recommend removing all water from the iron prior to ironing if the label has this symbol.

 TEMPERATURE SYMBOLS: The most common temperature symbols are one dot, two dots, and three dots; however, four and five dots are sometimes shown. One dot is for ironing on a low temperature (275°F, or 135°C), two is for medium temperature (325°F, or 160°C), and three is for high temperature (400°F, or 200°C). These dots denote similar ascending temperatures in the washing and drying symbols but do not equate to the same temperatures.

Dry – Cleaning Symbols

The Dry Clean symbol is denoted as a circle, which can sometimes be confused with the Normal Tumble Dry symbol. We too are annoyed by it not being another shape. Why not a pentagon? A rhombus? A star? A heart?

DRY CLEAN: This symbol has a circle and means that the item can be dry-cleaned.

DO NOT DRY CLEAN: This is the Dry Clean symbol with an X through it. Simply put, do not dry clean; the item will likely be damaged if dry-cleaned.

WET CLEAN: This is the Dry Clean symbol with a W inside it and means that the item can be wet-cleaned (cleaned with a professional water-based process).

DO NOT WET CLEAN: This is the Dry Clean symbol filled in with black and has an X through it. The item cannot be wet-cleaned.

Note: There are many dry-cleaning symbols that are only relevant to the dry cleaner and do not mean anything to you. The only part you need to understand is if the item can or cannot be dry-cleaned. If you're curious, ask your dry cleaner what it means or what they recommend.

THE A-TO-Z STAIN REMOVAL GUIDE

ach stain requires different types of stain-removal products and processes. We have organized all types of stains alphabetically into four categories—stain type, removal difficulty, what you will need, and removal instructions—to make the chore a bit easier to understand and deal with.

Animal Fats

TYPE: Greasy, Enzymatic

DIFFICULTY: Moderate

WHAT YOU WILL NEED: Dish soap or laundry detergent, soft-bristle brush, all-purpose stain-remover spray (with the enzyme lipase)

1. Mix a solution of 2 or 3 drops of dish soap or laundry detergent and 1 cup (240 ml) of warm water. Work this solution into the stain and tamp it in with the brush.

2. Tamp or pat in the all-purpose stain remover (the enzyme needed to break down animal fat is lipase) with the brush.

3. Allow these pretreatments to sit on the stain for at least 15 minutes.

4. Wash as recommended on the care label.

5. Inspect before drying. If the stain was removed, dry as recommended on the care label; if not, repeat steps 1 and 2 and allow the pretreatment to sit on the stain overnight prior to rewashing.

6. Rewash on a warm or high water temperature.

Ash

TYPE: Particulate

DIFFICULTY: Moderate

WHAT YOU WILL NEED: Soft-bristle brush, baking and/or washing soda

1. Wipe or gently brush away any physical bits of the remaining stain.

2. Create a paste of equal parts water and baking or washing soda. Work this solution into the stain with the brush and allow the pretreatment to sit for 15 minutes.

3. Add ¼ cup (30 g) of washing or baking soda into the tub of your washing machine
and wash as recommended on the care label.

4. Inspect before drying. If the stain was removed, dry as recommended on the care label; if not, repeat steps 2 and 3.

5. If the odor and stain remain, take your garment to a dry cleaner. Dry-cleaning solvent excels at removing ash, soot, and smoke stains and odors.

Avocado

TYPE: Combination (Enzymatic and Oxidizable/Bleachable)

DIFFICULTY: Moderate

WHAT YOU WILL NEED: Dish soap or laundry detergent, soft-bristle brush, all-purpose stain-remover spray (with the enzyme lipase)

1. Mix a solution of 2 or 3 drops of dish soap or laundry detergent and 1 cup (240 ml) of warm water. Work this solution into the stain and tamp it in with the brush.

2. Tamp or pat in the all-purpose stain remover (the enzyme needed to break down animal fats/oils is lipase) with the brush.

3. Allow these pretreatments to sit on the stain for at least 15 minutes.

4. Wash as recommended on the care label.

5. Inspect before drying. If the stain was removed, dry as recommended on the care label; if not, repeat steps 1 and 2 and allow the pretreatment to sit on the stain overnight prior to rewashing.

6. Rewash on a warm or high water temperature.

Baby Food

TYPE: Enzymatic

DIFFICULTY: Easy

WHAT YOU WILL NEED: Clean towel or soft-bristle brush, all-purpose stain remover (with the enzyme amylase), powdered oxygen bleach or 3% hydrogen peroxide (as needed)

1. Wipe, rinse, or gently brush away any physical bits of the remaining stain with the towel or brush.

2. Treat with the all-purpose stain remover (the enzyme needed to break down carbohydrates is amylase).

3. Work the stain remover into the stain for better results and wait at least 15 minutes before washing.

4. Wash as recommended on the care label.

5. Inspect before drying. If the stain was removed, dry as recommended on the care label; if not, repeat steps 2 and 3 OR follow step 6.

6. Soak in hot water and powdered oxygen bleach for at least 8 hours or overnight (see the Soaking section on page 65) OR spray the soiled areas with 3% hydrogen peroxide and allow to air-dry.

7. Rewash and inspect before drying.

Barbecue Sauce

TYPE: Enzymatic

DIFFICULTY: Moderate

WHAT YOU WILL NEED: Dish soap or laundry detergent, soft-bristle brush, all-purpose stain-remover spray (with the enzyme amylase), powdered oxygen bleach or 3% hydrogen peroxide (as needed)

1. Wipe or rinse away any physical bits of the remaining stain.

2. Mix a solution of 2 or 3 drops of dish soap or laundry detergent and 1 cup (240 ml) of warm water. Work this solution into the stain and tamp it in with the brush.

3. Tamp or pat in the all-purpose stain remover (the enzyme needed to break down sugar is amylase) with the brush.

4. Allow these pretreatments to sit on the stain for at least 15 minutes.

5. Wash as recommended by the care label.

6. Inspect before drying. If the stain was removed, dry as recommended by the care label; if the stain was not removed, repeat steps 2 and 3 and allow the pretreatment to sit on the stain overnight prior to rewashing.

7. Rewash on a warm or high water temperature.

8. If the stain remains, soak it in hot water and powdered oxygen bleach for at least 8 hours or overnight (see the Soaking section on page 65) OR spray the soiled areas with 3% hydrogen peroxide and allow to air-dry.

9. Rewash and inspect before drying.

Beer

TYPE: Oxidizable/Bleachable

DIFFICULTY: Easy

WHAT YOU WILL NEED: Powdered oxygen bleach or 3% hydrogen peroxide (as needed)

1. Rinse the stain with warm water as soon as possible.

2. Wash as recommended on the care label.

3. Inspect before drying. If the stain was removed, dry as recommended on the care label; if not, follow steps 4 and 5.

4. Soak it in hot water and powdered oxygen bleach for at least 8 hours or overnight (see the Soaking section on page 65) OR spray the soiled areas with 3% hydrogen peroxide and allow to air-dry.

5. Rewash and inspect before drying.

Beetroot

TYPE: Oxidizable/Bleachable

DIFFICULTY: Moderate

WHAT YOU WILL NEED: Powdered oxygen bleach or 3% hydrogen peroxide (as needed)

The main cause of a beetroot stain is red pigment. You will need to use a form of bleach; we recommend oxygen bleach to remove this stain.

1. Wipe or gently brush away any physical bits of the remaining stain.

2. Soak it in hot water and powdered oxygen bleach for at least 8 hours or overnight (see the Soaking section on page 65) OR spray the soiled areas with 3% hydrogen peroxide and allow to air-dry.

3. Wash as recommended on the care label.

4. Inspect before drying. If the stain was removed, dry as recommended on the care label; if not, repeat steps 2 and 3.

Shop Talk TANNINS

Tannins in plants occupy up to 20 percent of the dry weight. The synthesis of tannins in plants is often associated with defense responses against microbial pathogens, harmful insects, herbivores, and UV radiation. Tannins are usually the reason for the brilliant color of most berries (strawberries, blueberries, grapes, etc.). The major class of tannins in blueberries are proanthocyanidins.

Berries

TYPE: Oxidizable/Bleachable

DIFFICULTY: Moderate

WHAT YOU WILL NEED: Clean towel or soft-bristle brush, cleaning vinegar (at least 20%), powdered oxygen bleach or 3% hydrogen peroxide (as needed)

1. Wipe, rinse, or gently brush away any physical bits of the remaining stain with the towel or brush.

2. Treat the stained area with enough cleaning vinegar to cover the stain and let sit for 1 hour. If you do not have cleaning vinegar, you can use distilled white vinegar 5%, but it will be less effective.

3. Wash as recommended on the care label.

4. Inspect before drying. If the stain was removed, dry as recommended on the care label; if not, follow steps 5 and 6.

5. If the stain remains, soak it in hot water and powdered oxygen bleach for at least 8 hours or overnight (see the Soaking section on page 65) OR spray the soiled areas with 3% hydrogen peroxide and allow to air-dry.

6. Rewash and inspect before drying.

Blood

TYPE: Enzymatic

DIFFICULTY: Moderate

WHAT YOU WILL NEED: 3% hydrogen peroxide, all-purpose stain-remover spray (with the enzyme protease) (as needed), powdered oxygen bleach

1. Rinse the stain with cold water as soon as possible.

2. Pretreat the stain with 3% hydrogen peroxide; this reaction should cause a white bubbling foam to appear.

3. Wash as recommended on the care label.

4. Inspect before tumble drying. If the stain was removed, dry as recommended on the care label; if not, follow steps 5 and 6.

5. Pretreat the stain with the all-purpose stain remover (the enzyme needed to break down protein is protease). Allow the pretreatment to sit on the stain for at least 1 hour.

6. Wash as recommended on the care label.

7. If the stain remains, soak it in hot water and powdered oxygen bleach for at least 8 hours or overnight (see the Soaking section on page 65) OR spray the soiled areas with 3% hydrogen peroxide and allow to air-dry.

8. Rewash and inspect before drying.

Body Odor

TYPE: Special (microbial)

DIFFICULTY: Varies

WHAT YOU WILL NEED: Stain-remover spray designed for odor removal, laundry detergent designed for odor removal, washing boosters (baking soda, washing soda, water softener, and/or sodium percarbonate), laundry sanitizing products, and oxygen bleach (it must be designated for sanitizing or odor removal)

Before we start, you should know that body odor is not really your fault and, contrary to popular belief, sweat is naturally almost entirely odorless. Our sweat glands secrete an oily fluid composed of proteins, lipids, and steroids. The odor comes from bacteria that live on our skin and produce malodor after they eat up our sweat. This is typically most notable at our armpits, which offer a moist, warm environment where microbes can thrive. To combat this, here is what we recommend:

1. Pretreat those stinky areas with the stain-remover spray designed for odor removal. The longer this pretreatment sits on the malodor, the better it will work.

2. Use a detergent especially designed for odor removal.

3. Add washing boosters into the tub of the washing machine before loading your clothes to make the detergent more effective; ¼ cup (30 g) will do.

4. Add a low pH rinse or sanitizing products (page 154) to the fabric softener compartment and ensure the fabric softener option is turned on (it goes in this specific compartment because it is dispensed at the end of the cleaning cycle).

5. Wash your items as recommended on the care label.

continued

6. If odor remains, soak your garments for at least 8 hours or overnight in hot water and a powdered sanitizing or odor removal product (see the Soaking section on page 65).

7. Rewash your items at a higher temperature.

Pro Tip   AVOID USING FABRIC SOFTENER

Fabric softener can trap body oils, which are what bacteria love to eat. We also recommend avoiding perfume products, like scent beads, until you have figured out how to remove the odor; otherwise, it may be hard for you to distinguish if the problem is actually solved or if you have just covered it up.

Bronzer

TYPE: Oxidizable/Bleachable

DIFFICULTY: Moderate

WHAT YOU WILL NEED: Dish soap or laundry detergent, soft-bristle brush, powdered oxygen bleach or 3% hydrogen peroxide (as needed)

1. Rinse the stain with cold water as soon as possible.

2. Mix a solution of 2 or 3 drops of dish soap or laundry detergent and 1 cup (240 ml) of warm water. Work this solution into the stain and tamp it in with the brush.

3. Wash as recommended on the care label.

4. Inspect before drying. If the stain was removed, dry as recommended on the care label; if not, follow steps 5 and 6.

5. If the stain remains, soak it in hot water and powdered oxygen bleach for at least 8 hours or overnight (see the Soaking section on page 65) OR spray the soiled areas with 3% hydrogen peroxide and allow to air-dry.

6. Rewash and inspect before drying.

Chocolate

TYPE: Enzymatic, Greasy

DIFFICULTY: Moderate

WHAT YOU WILL NEED: Dish soap or laundry detergent, soft-bristle brush, all-purpose stain-remover spray (with the enzymes lipase, amylase, and protease)

Chocolate can be a surprisingly difficult stain to remove because it includes fat, tannins, sugar, and protein, which makes it quite complex.

1. Mix a solution of 2 or 3 drops of dish soap or laundry detergent and 1 cup (240 ml) of warm water. Work this solution into the stain and tamp it in with the brush.

2. Tamp or pat in the all-purpose stain remover (the enzymes needed to break down the fats, sugars, and protein are lipase, amylase, and protease) with the brush.

3. Allow both pretreatments to sit on the stain for at least 15 minutes.

4. Wash as recommended on the care label.

5. Inspect before drying. If the stain was removed, dry as recommended on the care label. If not, repeat steps 1 and 2 and allow the pretreatments to sit on the stain overnight prior to rewashing.

6. Rewash on a warm or high water temperature.

Coffee

TYPE: Oxidizable/Bleachable

DIFFICULTY: Easy

WHAT YOU WILL NEED: Powdered oxygen bleach or 3% hydrogen peroxide (as needed)

1. Rinse the stain with cold water as soon as possible.

2. Soak it in hot water and powdered oxygen bleach for at least 8 hours or overnight (see the Soaking section on page 65) OR spray the soiled areas with 3% hydrogen peroxide and allow to air-dry.

3. Wash as recommended on the care label.

4. Inspect before drying. If the stain was removed, dry as recommended on the care label; if not, repeat steps 2 and 3.

Cranberry

TYPE: Oxidizable/Bleachable

DIFFICULTY: Easy

WHAT YOU WILL NEED: Powdered oxygen bleach or 3% hydrogen peroxide (as needed)

1. Rinse the stain with cold water as soon as possible.

2. Soak it in hot water and powdered oxygen bleach for at least 8 hours or overnight (see the Soaking section on page 65) OR spray the soiled areas with 3% hydrogen peroxide and allow to air-dry.

3. Wash as recommended on the care label.

4. Inspect before drying. If the stain was removed, dry as recommended on the care label; if not, repeat steps 2 and 3.

Crayon

TYPE: Special (wax)

DIFFICULTY: Moderate

WHAT YOU WILL NEED: Clean towels, rubbing alcohol (isopropyl alcohol), laundry detergent or dish soap, hair dryer (as needed)

1. Place a clean towel behind the stain.

2. Pour 1 teaspoon of the rubbing alcohol onto another clean towel. Blot the stain; do NOT rub. The stain should transfer to the two towels.

3. Rub laundry detergent or dish soap into the stain and wait 15 minutes before washing.

4. Wash as recommended on the care label.

5. Inspect before drying. If the stain was removed, dry as recommended on the care label; if not, follow steps 6 and 7.

6. Repeat step 2 but heat up the stain first with the hair dryer and then rewash.

7. Inspect before drying. If the stain was removed, dry as recommended by the care label; if not, follow step 8.

8. Get this garment dry-cleaned. Dry-cleaning solvent makes wax stain removal quite easy.

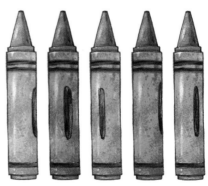

Curry

TYPE: Greasy, Oxidizable/Bleachable

DIFFICULTY: Hard

WHAT YOU WILL NEED: Powdered oxygen bleach or 3% hydrogen peroxide, all-purpose stain-remover spray (with the enzyme lipase)

Curry stains are one of the most challenging to remove. This oxygen bleach process may require 4 or 5 repetitions before the color is finally removed.

1. Wipe, rinse, or gently brush away any physical bits of the remaining stain.

2. Soak it in hot water and powdered oxygen bleach for at least 8 hours or overnight (see the Soaking section on page 65) OR spray the soiled areas with 3% hydrogen peroxide and allow to air-dry. (Once you add oxygen bleach to the stain, it will turn from yellow to red. Turmeric, which is responsible for the yellow color in curry, contains a chemical called curcumin, which will turn red when exposed to alkaline solutions, such as oxygen bleach.)

3. Treat with the all-purpose stain remover (the enzyme needed to break down a grease stain is lipase).

4. Allow this pretreatment to sit on the stain for at least 15 minutes.

5. Wash as recommended on the care label.

6. Inspect before drying. If the stain was removed, dry as recommended on the care label. If not, repeat steps 2 and 5.

Deodorant

TYPE: Special

DIFFICULTY: Moderate

WHAT YOU WILL NEED: Clean towel and/or soft-bristle brush, dish soap, rust stain remover (with citric or oxalic acid to neutralize the rust)

Deodorant is actually a rust/corrosion stain due to the metals in most formulations. This is why a stain remover specifically for rust stains is so important.

1. Wipe, rinse, or gently brush away any physical bits of the remaining deodorant with the towel or the brush.

2. Mix a solution of 2 or 3 drops of dish soap and 1 cup (240 ml) of warm water. Work this solution into the stain and tamp it in with the brush.

3. Tamp or pat in the rust stain remover with the brush.

4. Allow this pretreatment to sit on the stain for at least 15 minutes.

5. Wash as recommended on the care label.

6. Inspect before drying. If the stain was removed, dry as recommended on the care label; if not, repeat steps 2 through 5.

Egg

TYPE: Enzymatic

DIFFICULTY: Easy

WHAT YOU WILL NEED: Clean towel and/or soft-bristle brush, all-purpose stain-remover spray (with the enzyme protease)

1. Wipe, rinse, or gently brush away any physical bits of the remaining stain with the towel or brush.

2. Tamp or pat in the all-purpose stain remover (the enzyme needed to break down the protein in egg is protease) with the brush.

3. Allow this pretreatment to sit on the stain for at least 15 minutes.

4. Wash as recommended on the care label.

5. Inspect before drying. If the stain was removed, dry as recommended on the care label; if not, repeat steps 2 through 4.

Feces

TYPE: Special

DIFFICULTY: Moderate

WHAT YOU WILL NEED: Gloves, all-purpose stain remover, high-quality laundry detergent, laundry sanitizing products, washing boosters (baking soda, washing soda, water softener, and/or sodium percarbonate), oxygen bleach (it must be designated for sanitizing) or chlorine bleach

The composition of human feces is roughly 75 percent water and 25 percent solid waste, including cellular lining, plant fibers, fats, proteins, mucus, bile, and other substances your body can't digest (i.e., an invisible galaxy of microbes—bacteria, viruses, archaea—both living and dead). The solid waste is what we focus on, as most of the water waste washes out easily. The possibly harmful bacteria and viruses present in feces, especially if the person is unwell, must be sanitized properly. First, we highly recommend researching the products you use to ensure the EPA has registered them to eliminate bacteria and viruses.

ALL-PURPOSE ENZYMATIC STAIN REMOVER: This will help break down any remaining fats, proteins, and food within the feces stain.

HIGH-QUALITY LAUNDRY DETERGENT, WITH "OXI" IN THE NAME: This will provide better cleaning results when it comes to killing bacteria and viruses.

LAUNDRY SANITIZING PRODUCTS: These are usually added to the fabric softener compartment of the washing machine and then dispensed during the rinse cycle. Do not mix these products with your detergent or put them in the tub of the machine; they must be added at the end. Laundry sanitizing products are specifically designed, and certified, to disinfect and kill germs. (Laundry detergents never claim to kill germs.) These products are few and far between; we only know of three that exist at the publication of this book, so we suggest doing some research on available products.

POWDERED WASHING BOOSTERS: These will help soften (negate minerals) and increase the pH of the wash water, which will allow your laundry detergent to work more efficiently (see page 28 for more information).

BLEACH, SUCH AS AN OXYGEN OR CHLORINE BLEACH DESIGNATED FOR SANITIZING: This requires soaking in hot water, ideally above 140°F (60°C).

Once you've gathered your products, follow this process:

1. Wearing gloves, rinse the item in warm water to remove as much of the physical stain as possible.

2. Pretreat the soiled areas with the all-purpose stain remover and wait at least 1 hour.

3. Add the high-quality detergent, sanitizing products, and washing boosters to your washing machine, then wash the soiled items in the hottest water possible (190°F, or 90°C). We recommend using the Sanitize cycle.

4. After washing, soak your items in bleach (oxygen OR chlorine) and hot water (see the Soaking section on page 65), ideally above 140°F, or 60°C.

5. Rewash (a Normal cycle will do here) or rinse your items to remove any remaining bleach.

6. Dry your clothing on a high temperature.

While this guide may seem cumbersome, you may not need to use every product and follow every step as listed. We provided a comprehensive guide to handle the worst-possible feces stain. For example, if this is a routine stain that you are handling often (like if you're a new parent), you can probably skip the bleaching steps; however, if someone is unwell in your home, we recommend following this guide closely.

Foundation

TYPE: Combination (Greasy, Particulate), but actually Special

DIFFICULTY: Hard

WHAT YOU WILL NEED: Old clean towel, micellar water, a rounded, rigid plastic tool (like the opposite end of a plastic utensil or a pen clip; we dry cleaners use a spotting bone)

1. Place a clean towel behind the stain.

2. Pour micellar water onto the stain so that the entire stained area is covered.

3. Using the rounded plastic tool, press and rub the stain so that it transfers onto the backing towel (the foundation's color should be transferring to the towel).

4. If the stain remains, move the stained area to a clean part of the backing towel and repeat the process.

5. Wash as recommended on the care label.

6. Foundation stains can be very difficult to remove. If the stain remains, bring the garment to a dry cleaner. Dry cleaners have access to special "dry-side" solvents that should provide much better results compared to at-home remedies.

Shop Talk   MICELLAR WATER

Micellar water is a skincare product that has gained popularity for its ability to effectively cleanse the skin without stripping away its natural oils. It consists of tiny oil molecules, called micelles, suspended in soft water. These micelles attract dirt, oil, and makeup, effectively removing them from the skin and fabric.

Fruit Juice

TYPE: Oxidizable/Bleachable

DIFFICULTY: Easy

WHAT YOU WILL NEED: Cleaning vinegar (at least 20%), powdered oxygen bleach or 3% hydrogen peroxide (as needed)

Most fruit juices are highly acidic, so to remove these stains, you will need to use an acid to help remove it from your garment. The most common and easy-to-use acid is cooking and cleaning vinegar.

1. Rinse the stain with cold water as soon as possible.

2. Treat the stained area with enough cleaning vinegar to cover the stain and let sit for 1 hour. The solution should turn the color of the fruit juice.

3. Wash as recommended on the care label. If you do not have cleaning vinegar, you can use distilled white vinegar 5%, but it will be less effective.

4. Inspect before drying. If the stain was removed, dry as recommended on the care label; if not, follow steps 5 and 6.

5. Soak it in hot water and powdered oxygen bleach for at least 8 hours or overnight (see the Soaking section on page 65) OR spray the soiled areas with 3% hydrogen peroxide and allow to air-dry.

6. Rewash and inspect before drying.

Glue (Gorilla and Krazy)

TYPE: Special

DIFFICULTY: Hard

WHAT YOU WILL NEED: Clean towels, nail polish remover (acetone), rubbing alcohol (isopropyl alcohol), laundry detergent

1. Place a clean towel behind the stain.

2. Pour 1 teaspoon of the nail polish remover onto another clean towel. Blot the stain; do NOT rub. The stain should transfer to the two towels

3. Pour 1 teaspoon of the rubbing alcohol onto a clean part of the top towel. Blot the stain; do NOT rub. The stain should transfer to the two towels.

4. Rub laundry detergent into the stain and wait 15 minutes before washing.

5. Wash as recommended on the care label.

6. Inspect before drying. If the stain was removed, dry as recommended on the care label; if not, follow step 8.

7. Get this garment dry-cleaned. Dry cleaners have access to special stain removers and will have much more success than with at-home remedies.

Grass

TYPE: Enzymatic

DIFFICULTY: Moderate

WHAT YOU WILL NEED: Clean towel and/or soft-bristle brush, all-purpose stain-remover spray (with the enzyme protease), powdered oxygen bleach or 3% hydrogen peroxide (as needed)

1. Wipe, rinse, or gently brush away any physical bits of the remaining stain with the towel or brush.

2. Tamp or pat in the all-purpose stain remover (the enzyme needed to break down the protein in grass is protease) with the brush.

3. Allow this pretreatment to sit on the stain for 15 minutes.

4. Wash as recommended on the care label.

5. Inspect before drying. If the stain was removed, dry as recommended on the care label. If not, follow steps 6 and 7.

6. Soak the stained garment in hot water and powdered oxygen bleach for at least 8 hours or overnight (see the Soaking section on page 65) OR spray the soiled areas with 3% hydrogen peroxide and allow to air-dry.

7. Rewash and inspect before drying.

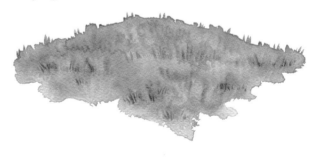

Grass and Mud

TYPE: Enzymatic, Particulate

DIFFICULTY: Hard

WHAT YOU WILL NEED: Clean towel and/or soft-bristle brush, all-purpose stain-remover spray (with the enzyme protease), washing or baking soda, powdered oxygen bleach or 3% hydrogen peroxide (as needed)

Grass combined with mud stains is one of the most challenging stains to remove. This process may require 4 or 5 repetitions before the color is finally removed.

1. Wipe, rinse, or gently brush away any physical bits of the remaining stain with the towel or brush.

2. Tamp or pat in the all-purpose stain remover (the enzyme needed to break down the protein in grass is protease) with the brush.

3. Create a paste of equal parts warm water and washing or baking soda. Work this solution into the stain.

4. Allow both pretreatments to sit on the stain for 15 minutes.

5. Add ¼ cup (30 g) of washing or baking soda to the tub of your washing machine and wash as recommended on the care label.

6. Inspect before drying. If the stain was removed, dry as recommended on the care label. If not, repeat steps 2 through 5 OR follow steps 7 and 8.

7. If the stain remains, soak it in hot water and powdered oxygen bleach for at least 8 hours or overnight (see the Soaking section on page 65) OR spray the soiled areas with 3% hydrogen peroxide and allow to air-dry.

8. Rewash and inspect before drying.

Gravy

TYPE: Enzymatic, Greasy

DIFFICULTY: Moderate

WHAT YOU WILL NEED: Dish soap or laundry detergent, soft-bristle brush, all-purpose stain-remover spray (with the enzymes protease and lipase)

1. Work 2 or 3 drops of dish soap or laundry detergent into the stain and tamp it in with the brush.

2. Tamp or pat in the all-purpose stain remover (the enzyme needed to break down a protein stain is protease; for a grease stain it's lipase) with the brush.

3. Allow both pretreatments to sit on the stain for at least 15 minutes.

4. Wash as recommended on the care label.

5. Inspect before drying. If the stain was removed, dry as recommended on the care label; if not, repeat steps 1 and 2 and allow the pretreatments to sit on the stain overnight prior to rewashing.

6. Rewash on a warm or high water temperature.

Grease

TYPE: Greasy

DIFFICULTY: Easy

WHAT YOU WILL NEED: Dish soap or laundry detergent, soft-bristle brush

1. Mix a solution of 2 or 3 drops of dish soap or laundry detergent and 1 cup (240 ml) of warm water. Work this solution into the stain and tamp it in with the brush.

2. Allow the pretreatment to sit on the stain for at least 15 minutes.

3. Wash as recommended on the care label.

4. Inspect before drying. If you dry a grease stain with heat, you may "set" the stain, which will make it much harder to remove. If the stain was removed, dry as recommended on the care label; If not, repeat step 1 and allow the pretreatment to sit on the stain overnight prior to rewashing.

5. Rewash on a warm or high water temperature.

Hot Sauce

TYPE: Oxidizable/Bleachable

DIFFICULTY: Hard

WHAT YOU WILL NEED: Cleaning vinegar (at least 20%), powdered oxygen bleach or 3% hydrogen peroxide (as needed)

Most hot sauce stains can be very challenging to remove because the red pigment is concentrated, and the sauce is highly acidic. To treat these stains, you will need to use an acid to help remove them from your garment. The most common and easy-to-use acid is vinegar.

1. Rinse the stain with cold water as soon as possible.

2. Treat the stained area with enough cleaning vinegar to cover the stain and let sit for 1 hour. If you do not have cleaning vinegar, you can use distilled white vinegar 5%, but it will be less effective.

3. Wash as recommended on the care label.

4. Inspect before drying. If the stain was removed, dry as recommended on the care label; if not, follow steps 5 and 6.

5. Soak it in hot water and powdered oxygen bleach for at least 8 hours or overnight (see the Soaking section on page 65) OR spray the soiled areas with 3% hydrogen peroxide and allow to air-dry.

6. Rewash and inspect before drying. If the stain is still not out, repeat steps 2 through 5.

Ink Stain

TYPE: Special

DIFFICULTY: Hard/Impossible

WHAT YOU WILL NEED: Old clean towels (see note in step 2), nail polish remover (acetone), rubbing alcohol (isopropyl alcohol), ink stain remover, laundry detergent

1. Put a clean towel behind the stain.

2. Pour 1 teaspoon of the nail polish remover onto another towel. Blot the stain; do NOT rub. The stain should transfer to the two towels. (Note: These towels will likely become ruined during the transfer process; do NOT use your best/favorite towels!)

3. Pour 1 teaspoon of the rubbing alcohol onto a clean part of the top towel. Blot the stain; do NOT rub. The stain should transfer to the two towels.

4. Treat the stain with the ink stain remover and blot with a clean part of the top towel or a fresh towel.

5. Gently rub laundry detergent into the stain and wait 15 minutes before washing.

6. Wash as recommended on the care label.

7. Inspect before drying. If the stain was removed, dry as recommended on the care label; if not, follow step 8.

8. Get this garment dry-cleaned. Dry cleaners have access to special stain removers and will have much more success than with at-home remedies.

Ketchup

TYPE: Enzymatic

DIFFICULTY: Easy

WHAT YOU WILL NEED: Clean towel and/or soft-bristle brush, all-purpose stain-remover spray (with the enzyme amylase), powdered oxygen bleach or 3% hydrogen peroxide

1. Wipe, rinse, or gently brush away any physical bits of the remaining stain with the towel or brush.

2. Tamp or pat in the all-purpose stain remover (the enzyme needed to break down the starch in tomato is amylase) with the brush.

3. Allow this pretreatment to sit on the stain for 15 minutes.

4. Wash as recommended on the care label.

5. Inspect before drying. If the stain was removed, dry as recommended on the care label; if not, follow steps 6 and 7.

6. Soak the stained garment in hot water and powdered oxygen bleach for at least 8 hours or overnight (see the Soaking section on page 65) OR spray the soiled areas with 3% hydrogen peroxide and allow to air-dry.

7. Rewash and inspect before drying.

Kimchi

TYPE: Oxidizable/Bleachable

DIFFICULTY: Hard

WHAT YOU WILL NEED: Clean towel or soft-bristle brush, powdered oxygen bleach or 3% hydrogen peroxide

Kimchi stains are one of the most challenging to remove. This process may require 4 or 5 repetitions before the color is finally removed.

1. Wipe, rinse, or gently brush away any physical bits of the remaining stain with the towel or brush.

2. Soak in hot water and powdered oxygen bleach for at least 8 hours or overnight (see the Soaking section on page 65) OR spray the soiled areas with 3% hydrogen peroxide and allow to air-dry.

3. Wash as recommended on the care label.

4. Inspect before drying. If the stain was removed, dry as recommended on the care label. If not, repeat steps 2 and 3.

Lipstick/Lip Gloss

TYPE: Combination (Greasy, Particulate), but actually Special

DIFFICULTY: Hard

WHAT YOU WILL NEED: Old clean towel, dish soap or high-quality laundry detergent, a rounded, rigid plastic tool (like the opposite end of a plastic utensil or a pen clip; we dry cleaners use a spotting bone)

1. Place a clean towel behind the stain.

2. Pour enough dish soap or laundry detergent onto the stain so that the entire stained area is covered.

3. Using the rounded plastic tool, press and rub the stain so that it transfers onto the backing towel (the lipstick's color should appear on the towel).

4. If the stain remains, move the stained area to a clean part of the backing towel and repeat the process.

5. Wash as recommended on the care label.

Mango

TYPE: Enzymatic

DIFFICULTY: Easy

WHAT YOU WILL NEED: Clean towel and/or soft-bristle brush, all-purpose stain-remover spray (with the enzyme amylase), powdered oxygen bleach or 3% hydrogen peroxide (as needed)

1. Wipe, rinse, or gently brush away any physical bits of the remaining stain with the towel or brush.

2. Tamp or pat in the all-purpose stain remover (the enzyme needed to break down the starch in mango is amylase) with the brush.

3. Allow this pretreatment to sit on the stain for 15 minutes.

4. Wash as recommended on the care label.

5. Inspect before drying. If the stain was removed, dry as recommended on the care label; if not, follow steps 6 and 7.

6. Soak it in hot water and powdered oxygen bleach for at least 8 hours or overnight (see the Soaking section on page 65) OR spray the soiled areas with 3% hydrogen peroxide and allow to air-dry.

7. Rewash and inspect before drying.

Mascara

TYPE: Combination (Greasy, Particulate), but actually Special
DIFFICULTY: Hard
WHAT YOU WILL NEED: Old clean towel, micellar water, a rounded, rigid plastic tool (like the opposite end of a plastic utensil or a pen clip; we dry cleaners use a spotting bone)

1. Place a clean towel behind the stain.

2. Pour micellar water onto the stain so that the entire stained area is covered.

3. Using your rounded plastic tool, press and rub the stain so it transfers onto the backing towel (the mascara's color should appear on the towel).

4. If the stain remains, move the stained area to a clean part of the backing towel and repeat the process.

5. Wash as recommended on the care label.

Maple Syrup

TYPE: Enzymatic
DIFFICULTY: Very easy

All you need to do is wash the item sooner rather than later—don't let it oxidize.

Meat Drippings

TYPE: Enzymatic, Greasy

DIFFICULTY: Moderate

WHAT YOU WILL NEED: Dish soap or laundry detergent, soft-bristle brush, all-purpose stain-remover spray (with the enzyme protease)

1. Mix a solution of 2 or 3 drops of dish soap or laundry detergent and 1 cup (240 ml) warm water. Work this solution into the stain and tamp it in with the brush.

2. Tamp or pat in the all-purpose stain remover (the enzyme needed to break down a protein stain is protease) with the brush.

3. Allow both pretreatments to sit on the stain for at least 15 minutes.

4. Wash as recommended on the care label.

5. Inspect before drying. If the stain was removed, dry as recommended on the care label; if not, repeat steps 1 and 2 and allow the pretreatments to sit on the stain overnight prior to rewashing.

6. Rewash on a warm or high water temperature.

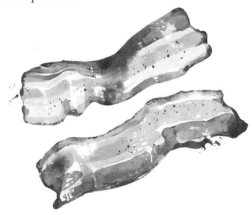

THE LAUNDRY BOOK

continued

Mildew (Mold)

TYPE: Special

DIFFICULTY: Moderate

WHAT YOU WILL NEED: Gloves, mask, mold-removal product (such as moldicide spray), high-quality laundry detergent, laundry sanitizing products, washing boosters (baking soda, washing soda, water softener), oxygen bleach (it must be designated for sanitizing), and chlorine bleach

Mold is tricky and the stain removal is a bit different from others as it requires specially formulated products to counteract mold and mold spores. Below, we outline why each product is useful and the best ways to use them. (Disclaimer: Mold removal requires the use of specifically formulated products, as mold and mold spores can be incredibly difficult to kill and remove. We do NOT recommend using DIY/at-home methods with common household products; they will not provide proper results.) First, we highly recommend researching a product to ensure the EPA has registered it to eliminate and prevent mold:

MOLD REMOVAL SPRAY: This is ideal for treating moldy areas that you can actually see. Spray the mold with this product and allow it to sit for at least 1 hour before washing.

HIGH-QUALITY LAUNDRY DETERGENT, ESPECIALLY ONE WITH "OXI" INCLUDED IN THE NAME: This will provide better cleaning results when it comes to killing bacteria and viruses.

LAUNDRY SANITIZING PRODUCTS: These are usually added to the fabric softener compartment of the washing machine and then dispensed during the rinse cycle. Do not mix these products with your detergent or put them in the tub of the machine; they must be added at the end.

continued

POWDERED WASHING BOOSTERS: These will help soften (negate minerals) and increase the pH of the wash water, which will allow your laundry detergent to work more efficiently (see page 28 for more information on powdered washing boosters).

BLEACH, SUCH AS AN OXYGEN OR CHLORINE BLEACH DESIGNATED FOR SANITIZING: This requires soaking in hot water, ideally above 140°F (60°C).

Once you've sorted out your mold-removal products, follow this process:

1. Wearing gloves and a mask, pretreat moldy areas with the moldicide spray and wait at least 1 hour.

2. Add the high-quality detergent, laundry sanitizers, and washing boosters to your washing machine, then wash the soiled items in the hottest water possible (190°F, or 90°C). We recommend using the Sanitize cycle.

3. After washing, soak your items in bleach (oxygen OR chlorine) and hot water (see the Soaking section on page 65), ideally above 140°F (60°C).

4. Rewash (a Normal cycle will do here) or rinse your items to remove any remaining bleach.

5. Dry your clothing on a high temperature.

6. Leave the washing machine door and product-compartments drawer open when not in use; this will help prevent mold buildup within the machine.

Milk

TYPE: Enzymatic, Greasy

DIFFICULTY: Moderate

WHAT YOU WILL NEED: Dish soap or laundry detergent, soft-bristle brush, all-purpose stain-remover spray (with the enzyme protease)

1. Mix a solution of 2 or 3 drops of dish soap or laundry detergent and 1 cup (240 ml) of warm water. Work this solution into the stain and tamp it in with the brush.

2. Tamp or pat in the all-purpose stain remover (the enzyme needed to break down a protein stain is protease) with the brush.

3. Allow both pretreatments to sit on the stain for at least 15 minutes.

4. Wash as recommended on the care label.

5. Inspect before drying. If the stain was removed, dry as recommended on the care label; if not, repeat steps 1 and 2 and allow the pretreatments to sit on the stain overnight prior to rewashing.

6. Rewash on a warm or high water temperature.

Milk (Chocolate)

TYPE: Enzymatic, Greasy, Oxidizable

DIFFICULTY: Moderate

WHAT YOU WILL NEED: Dish soap or laundry detergent, soft-bristle brush, all-purpose stain-remover spray (with the enzymes lipase, amylase, and protease), powdered oxygen bleach or 3% hydrogen peroxide (as needed)

Chocolate milk stains can be surprisingly difficult to remove because it includes fat, tannins, and protein, which makes it quite complex!

1. Mix a solution of 2 or 3 drops of dish soap or laundry detergent and 1 cup (240 ml) of warm water. Work this solution into the stain and tamp it in with the brush.

2. Tamp or pat in the all-purpose stain remover (the enzymes needed to break down the fats, sugars, and protein in chocolate are lipase, amylase, and protease) with the brush.

3. Allow both pretreatments to sit on the stain for at least 15 minutes.

4. Wash as recommended on the care label.

5. Inspect before drying. If the stain was removed, dry as recommended on the care label; if not, repeat steps 1 and 2 and allow the pretreatments to sit on the stain overnight prior to rewashing.

6. Rewash on a warm or high water temperature.

7. If the stain's color is still present, soak it in hot water and powdered oxygen bleach overnight OR spray the garment with 3% hydrogen peroxide and allow it to air-dry.

8. Wash as recommended on the care label.

Molasses

TYPE: Enzymatic

DIFFICULTY: Moderate

WHAT YOU WILL NEED: Dish soap or laundry detergent, soft-bristle brush, all-purpose stain-remover spray (with the enzyme amylase), oxygen bleach (hydrogen peroxide or powdered oxygen bleach)

1. Wipe or rinse away any physical bits of the remaining stain.

2. Mix a solution of 2 or 3 drops of dish soap or laundry detergent and 1 cup (240 ml) of warm water. Work this solution into the stain and tamp it in with the brush.

3. Tamp or pat in the all-purpose stain remover (the enzyme needed to break down sugar is amylase) with the brush.

4. Allow both pretreatments to sit on the stain for at least 15 minutes.

5. Wash as recommended on the care label.

6. Inspect before drying. If the stain was removed, dry as recommended on the care label; if not, repeat steps 1 and 2 and allow the pretreatments to sit on the stain overnight prior to rewashing.

7. Rewash on a warm or high water temperature.

Mud

TYPE: Particulate

DIFFICULTY: Moderate

WHAT YOU WILL NEED: Washing or baking soda

1. If the stain is still wet, allow it to dry.

2. Wipe or gently brush away any physical bits of the remaining stain.

3. Create a paste of equal parts water and washing or baking soda. Work this solution into the stain.

4. Allow this pretreatment to sit on the stain for 15 minutes.

5. Add ¼ cup (30 g) of washing or baking soda to the tub of your washing machine and wash as recommended on the care label.

6. Inspect before drying. If the stain was removed, dry as recommended on the care label. If not, repeat steps 3 through 5.

Mustard

TYPE: Greasy, Oxidizable/Bleachable

DIFFICULTY: Hard

WHAT YOU WILL NEED: Clean towel and/or soft-bristle brush, powdered oxygen bleach or 3% hydrogen peroxide, all-purpose stain-remover spray (with the enzyme lipase)

Mustard stains are one of the most challenging to remove. The oxygen bleach process may require 4 or 5 repetitions before the color is finally removed.

1. Wipe, rinse, or gently brush away any physical bits of the remaining stain with the towel or brush.

2. Soak it in hot water and powdered oxygen bleach for at least 8 hours or overnight (see the Soaking section on page 65) OR spray the soiled areas with 3% hydrogen peroxide and allow to air-dry. (Once you add oxygen bleach to the stain, it will turn from yellow to red. Turmeric, which is responsible for the yellow color in mustard, contains a chemical called curcumin, which will turn red when exposed to alkaline solutions, such as oxygen bleach).

3. Tamp or pat in the all-purpose stain remover (the enzyme needed to break down a grease stain is lipase) with the brush.

4. Allow this pretreatment to sit on the stain for at least 15 minutes.

5. Wash as recommended on the care label.

6. Inspect before drying. If the stain was removed, dry as recommended on the care label. If not, repeat steps 2 and 5.

Nail Polish

TYPE: Special

DIFFICULTY: Hard/Impossible

WHAT YOU WILL NEED: Old clean towels (see note in step 2), nail polish remover (acetone), rubbing alcohol (isopropyl alcohol), laundry detergent

1. Place a clean towel behind the stain.

2. Pour 1 teaspoon of the nail polish remover onto a clean part of the top towel. Blot the stain; do NOT rub. The stain should transfer to the two towels. (Note: These towels will likely become ruined during the transfer process; do NOT use your best/favorite towels!)

3. Pour 1 teaspoon of the rubbing alcohol onto another towel. Blot the stain; do NOT rub. The stain should transfer to the two towels.

4. Gently rub laundry detergent into the stain and wait 15 minutes before washing.

5. Wash as recommended on the care label.

6. Inspect before drying. If the stain was removed, dry as recommended on the care label; if not, follow step 7.

7. Get this garment dry-cleaned. Dry cleaners have access to special stain removers and will have much more success than with at-home remedies.

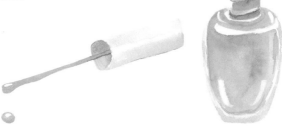

Olive Oil

TYPE: Greasy

DIFFICULTY: Easy

WHAT YOU WILL NEED: What you will need: Dish soap or laundry detergent, soft-bristle brush

1. Mix a solution of 2 or 3 drops of dish soap or laundry detergent and 1 cup (240 ml) of warm water. Work this solution into the stain and tamp it in with the brush.

2. Allow the pretreatment to sit on the stain for at least 15 minutes.

3. Wash as recommended on the care label.

4. Inspect before drying (if you dry a grease stain with heat, you may "set" the stain, which will make it much harder to remove). If the stain was removed, dry as recommended on the care label; If not, repeat steps 1 and allow the pretreatment to sit on the stain overnight prior to rewashing.

5. Rewash on a warm or high water temperature

Paint (Oil-Based)

TYPE: Combination (Greasy, Particulate), but actually Special
DIFFICULTY: Hard
WHAT YOU WILL NEED: Old clean towel, dish soap or high-quality laundry detergent, a rounded, rigid plastic tool (like the opposite end of a plastic utensil or a pen clip; we dry cleaners use a spotting bone), acetone

1. Place a clean towel behind the oil paint stain.

2. Pour enough dish soap or laundry detergent onto the stain so that the entire stained area is covered. Using the rounded plastic tool, press and rub the stain so that it transfers onto the backing towel (the paint's color should appear on the towel).

3. If the stain remains, move the stained area to a clean part of the backing towel and pour enough acetone so that the entire stain is covered. Using the rounded plastic tool, press and rub the stain so that it transfers onto the backing towel.

4. Wash as recommended on the care label.

Paint (Water – /Acrylic – Based)

TYPE: Combination (Greasy, Particulate), but actually Special
DIFFICULTY: Hard
WHAT YOU WILL NEED: Old clean towel, rubbing alcohol (isopropyl alcohol) or hand sanitizer, a rounded, rigid plastic tool (like the opposite end of a plastic utensil or a pen clip; we dry cleaners use a spotting bone)

1. Place a clean towel behind the stain.

2. Pour enough rubbing alcohol or hand sanitizer onto the stain so that the entire stained area is covered. Using the rounded plastic tool, press and rub the stain so that it transfers onto the backing towel (the paint's color should appear on the towel).

3. If the stain remains, move the stained area to a clean part of the backing towel and repeat the process. If you have both rubbing alcohol and hand sanitizer, use the one you have not tried yet. Using the rounded plastic tool, press and rub the stain so that it transfers onto the backing towel.

4. Wash as recommended on the care label.

Peanut Butter

TYPE: Enzymatic, Greasy
DIFFICULTY: Moderate
WHAT YOU WILL NEED: Clean towel, dish soap or laundry detergent, soft-bristle brush, all-purpose stain-remover spray (with the enzymes protease and amylase)

1. Allow the stain to dry and then wipe away any physical bits with a clean, damp towel.

2. Mix a solution of 2 or 3 drops of dish soap or laundry detergent and 1 cup (240 ml) of warm water. Work this solution into the stain and tamp it in with the brush.

3. Tamp or pat in the all-purpose stain remover (the enzymes needed to break down protein and sugar are protease and amylase) with the brush.

4. Allow both pretreatments to sit on the stain for at least 15 minutes.

5. Wash as recommended on the care label.

6. Inspect before drying. If the stain was removed, dry as recommended on the care label; if not, repeat steps 2 and 3 and allow the pretreatments to sit on the stain overnight prior to rewashing.

7. Rewash on a warm or high water temperature.

Permanent Marker (including Sharpie)

TYPE: Special

DIFFICULTY: Hard/Impossible

WHAT YOU WILL NEED: Old clean towels (see note in step 2), nail polish remover (acetone), rubbing alcohol (isopropyl alcohol), ink stain remover, laundry detergent

1. Place a clean towel behind the stain.

2. Pour 1 teaspoon of the nail polish remover onto another clean towel. Blot the stain; do NOT rub. The stain should transfer to the two towels. (Note: These towels will likely become ruined during the transfer process; do NOT use your best/favorite towels!)

3. Pour 1 teaspoon of the rubbing alcohol onto another clean towel. Blot the stain; do NOT rub. The stain should transfer to the two towels.

4. Treat the stain with the ink stain remover and blot with a fresh towel.

5. Rub laundry detergent into the stain and wait 15 minutes before washing.

6. Wash as recommended on the care label.

7. Inspect before drying. If the stain was removed, dry as recommended on the care label; if not, follow step 8.

8. Get this garment dry-cleaned. Dry cleaners have access to special stain removers and will have much more success than with at-home remedies.

Pet Urine

TYPE: Enzymatic

DIFFICULTY: Moderate

WHAT YOU WILL NEED: Clean towel (as needed), all-purpose enzymatic pet stain remover, soft-bristle brush, powdered oxygen bleach or 3% hydrogen peroxide (as needed), extraction machine (page 184)

FOR PET STAINS ON CLOTHING

1. Rinse stains with warm water or blot with water and a clean towel.

2. Tamp or pat in the enzymatic pet stain remover with the brush.

3. Allow this pretreatment to sit on the stain for 15 minutes.

4. Wash as recommended on the care label.

5. Inspect before drying. If the stain was removed, dry as recommended on the care label; if not, repeat steps 2 through 4.

6. If the stain remains, soak it in hot water and powdered oxygen bleach for at least 8 hours or overnight (see the Soaking section on page 65) OR spray the soiled areas with 3% hydrogen peroxide and allow to air-dry.

7. Rewash and inspect before drying.

FOR PET STAINS ON FURNITURE, RUGS, AND NON-MACHINE-WASHABLE TEXTILES

1. Blot (do NOT rub) the stain with warm water and a clean towel.

2. Tamp or pat in the enzymatic pet stain remover with the brush.

continued

3. Allow this pretreatment to sit on the stain for 15 minutes.

4. Use the extraction machine on the stain.

5. If the stain remains, repeat steps 2 through 4, allowing the pretreatment to sit on the stain overnight.

6. Once you are satisfied with the cleaning results, you can use 3% hydrogen peroxide to correct any remaining color; however, some pet stains cannot be corrected, as they can discolor fabrics.

Shop Talk EXTRACTION MACHINE

An extraction machine is an incredibly helpful and versatile appliance to have around the house (especially if you have pets or children). It sprays cleaning solution and then quickly removes, sucks, or extracts it from objects like furniture and rugs (it's basically a fancy wet vacuum that cleans). We recommend using a tiny amount of upholstery detergent with an extraction machine, as these products are concentrated (take it from us who have cleaned hundreds of pieces and added too much, which has caused quite a headache).

Red Wine

TYPE: Oxidizable/Bleachable

DIFFICULTY: Easy

WHAT YOU WILL NEED: Cleaning vinegar (at least 20%),
powdered oxygen bleach or 3% hydrogen peroxide (as needed)

Wine is highly acidic, so to remove this stain from your garment, you will need to use
an acid. The most common and easy-to-use acid is vinegar.

1. Rinse the stain with cold water as soon as possible.

2. Treat the stained area with enough cleaning vinegar to cover the stain and let
   sit for 1 hour. If you do not have cleaning vinegar, you can use distilled white
   vinegar 5%, but it will be less effective. The solution should turn the color of
   the wine.

3. Wash as recommended on the care label.

4. Inspect before drying. If the stain was removed, dry as recommended on the
   care label; if not, follow steps 5 and 6.

5. Soak the stained garment in hot water and powdered
   oxygen bleach for at least 8 hours or overnight (see the
   Soaking section on page 65) OR spray the soiled areas
   with 3% hydrogen peroxide and allow to air-dry.

6. Rewash and inspect before drying.

Rust

TYPE: Special

DIFFICULTY: Moderate

WHAT YOU WILL NEED: Clean towel and/or soft-bristle brush, rust stain remover

1. Wipe, rinse, or gently brush away any physical bits of the remaining stain with the towel or brush.

2. Tamp or pat in the rust stain remover with the brush

3. Allow this pretreatment to sit on the stain for at least 15 minutes.

4. Wash as recommended on the care label.

5. Inspect before drying. If the stain was removed, dry as recommended on the care label; if not, repeat steps 2 through 4.

6. If the stain remains, bring the garment to a dry cleaner. Dry cleaners have access to special rust stain removers (hydrofluoric acid) and will have much more success than with at-home remedies.

Salad Dressing

TYPE: Enzymatic, Greasy

DIFFICULTY: Moderate

WHAT YOU WILL NEED: Dish soap or laundry detergent, soft-bristle brush, all-purpose stain-remover spray (with the enzymes lipase, amylase, and protease), powdered oxygen bleach or 3% hydrogen peroxide (as needed)

1. Mix a solution of 2 or 3 drops of dish soap or laundry detergent and 1 cup (240 ml) of warm water. Work this solution into the stain and tamp it in with the brush.

2. Tamp or pat in the all-purpose stain remover (the enzymes needed to break down the fats, sugars, and protein are lipase, amylase, and protease) with the brush.

3. Allow both pretreatments to sit on the stain for at least 15 minutes.

4. Wash as recommended on the care label.

5. Inspect before drying. If the stain was removed, dry as recommended on the care label; if not, repeat steps 1 and 2 and allow the pretreatments to sit on the stain overnight prior to rewashing.

6. Rewash on a warm or high water temperature.

7. If the stain remains, soak it in hot water and powdered oxygen bleach for at least 8 hours or overnight (see the Soaking section on page 65) OR spray the soiled areas with 3% hydrogen peroxide and allow to air-dry.

8. Rewash and inspect before drying.

Smoke

TYPE: Particulate

DIFFICULTY: Moderate

WHAT YOU WILL NEED: Washing or baking soda

1. Wipe or gently brush away any physical bits of the remaining stain (this will likely be ash or soot).

2. Create a paste of equal parts water and washing or baking soda. Work this solution into the visibly stained areas and/or the areas with strong odors.

3. Allow this pretreatment to sit for 15 minutes.

4. Add ¼ cup (30 g) of the washing or baking soda into the tub of your washing machine and wash as recommended on the care label.

5. Inspect before drying. If the stain was removed, dry as recommended on the care label; if not, repeat steps 2 through 4.

6. If the smoke odor and stain still remain, take your garment to a dry cleaner. Dry-cleaning solvent excels at removing ash, soot, and smoke stains. Dry cleaners also have access to ozone treatments, which excel at removing smoke odors.

Soy Sauce

TYPE: Oxidizable/Bleachable

DIFFICULTY: Easy

WHAT YOU WILL NEED: Powdered oxygen bleach or 3% hydrogen peroxide

1. Rinse the stain with warm water as soon as possible. A soy sauce stain is much easier to remove if treated and cleaned within the first 24 hours.

2. Wash as recommended on the care label.

3. Inspect before drying. If the stain was removed, dry as recommended on the care label; if not, follow steps 4 and 5.

4. Soak it in hot water and powdered oxygen bleach for at least 8 hours or overnight (see the Soaking section on page 65) OR spray the soiled areas with 3% hydrogen peroxide and allow to air-dry.

5. Rewash and inspect before drying.

Sunscreen

TYPE: Special

DIFFICULTY: Moderate

WHAT YOU WILL NEED: What you will need: Rust stain remover, clean towel

1. Wipe, rinse, or gently brush away any physical bits of the remaining stain.

2. Treat with the rust stain remover. Allow this pretreatment to sit on the stain for at least 15 minutes

3. Wash as recommended on the care label.

4. Inspect before drying. If the stain was removed, dry as recommended on the care label; if not, repeat steps 2 and 3.

5. If the stain remains, bring the garment to a dry cleaner. Dry cleaners have access to special rust stain removers (hydrofluoric acid) and will have much more success than with at-home remedies.

Sweat (Oxidized Yellow Stain)

TYPE: Oxidizable/Bleachable

DIFFICULTY: Moderate

WHAT YOU WILL NEED: Powdered oxygen bleach or 3% hydrogen peroxide

For severely yellow/brown sweat stains, consider taking your garments to a dry cleaner. Dry cleaners have access to special stain removers and will have much more success than with at-home remedies.

1. Soak it in hot water and powdered oxygen bleach for at least 8 hours or overnight (see the Soaking section on page 65) OR spray the soiled areas with 3% hydrogen peroxide and allow it to air-dry.

2. Wash as recommended on the care label.

3. Inspect before drying. If the stain was removed, dry as recommended on the care label; if not, repeat steps 1 and 2.

Tea

TYPE: Oxidizable/Bleachable

DIFFICULTY: Easy

WHAT YOU WILL NEED: Powdered oxygen bleach or 3% hydrogen peroxide

1. Soak it in hot water and powdered oxygen bleach for at least 8 hours or overnight (see the Soaking section on page 65) OR spray the soiled areas with 3% hydrogen peroxide and allow to air-dry.

2. Wash as recommended on the care label.

3. Inspect before drying. If the stain was removed, dry as recommended on the care label; if not, repeat steps 1 and 2.

Tomato Sauce

TYPE: Enzymatic, Greasy

DIFFICULTY: Moderate/Hard

WHAT YOU WILL NEED: Dish soap or laundry detergent, soft-bristle brush, all-purpose stain-remover spray (with the enzymes lipase and amylase), powdered oxygen bleach or 3% hydrogen peroxide (as needed)

Tomato sauce stains can be very challenging to remove on lighter-colored garments. This oxygen bleach process may require 4 or 5 repetitions before the color is finally removed.

1. Mix a solution of 2 or 3 drops of dish soap or laundry detergent and 1 cup (240 ml) of warm water. Work this solution into the stain and tamp it in with the brush.

2. Tamp or pat in the all-purpose stain remover (the enzymes needed to break down fat and sugar are lipase and amylase) with the brush.

3. Allow both pretreatments to sit on the stain for at least 15 minutes.

4. Wash as recommended on the care label.

5. Inspect before drying. If the stain was removed, dry as recommended on the care label; if not, follow steps 6 and 7.

6. Soak it in hot water and powdered oxygen bleach for at least 8 hours or overnight (see the Soaking section on page 65) OR spray the soiled areas with 3% hydrogen peroxide and allow to air-dry.

7. Rewash and inspect before drying.

Urine

TYPE: Enzymatic

DIFFICULTY: Easy

WHAT YOU WILL NEED: All-purpose stain-remover spray (with the enzyme protease), soft-bristle brush, ammonia, powdered oxygen bleach or 3% hydrogen peroxide (as needed)

1. Rinse the stain in warm water as soon as possible to remove as much water content as you can.

2. Tamp or pat in the all-purpose stain remover (the enzyme needed to break down the protein and waste in urine is protease) with the brush.

3. Allow this pretreatment to sit on the stain for 15 minutes.

4. Add ½ cup (120 ml) of ammonia to the tub of your washing machine before adding the clothes. Wash as recommended on the care label.

5. Inspect before drying. If the stain was removed, dry as recommended on the care label; if not, follow steps 6 and 7.

6. Soak it in hot water and powdered oxygen bleach for at least 8 hours or overnight (see the Soaking section on page 65) OR spray the soiled areas with 3% hydrogen peroxide and allow to air-dry.

7. Rewash and inspect before drying.

Vomit

TYPE: Special, but mostly Enzymatic

DIFFICULTY: Moderate/Hard

WHAT YOU WILL NEED: Clean towel and/or soft-bristle brush, all-purpose stain-remover spray (with enzymes depending on the food consumed), powdered oxygen bleach or 3% hydrogen peroxide (as needed)

Vomit stains will vary greatly depending on what was consumed prior to getting sick. We recommend following the stain removal guide for whatever is included in the regurgitation. Unfortunately, stomach acids are quite strong and may cause discolorations similar to chlorine bleach, which are not correctable.

1. Wipe, rinse, or gently brush away any physical bits of the remaining stain with the towel or brush.

2. Tamp or pat in the all-purpose stain with the brush.

3. Allow this pretreatment to sit on the stain for 15 minutes.

4. Wash as recommended on the care label.

5. Inspect before drying. If the stain was removed, dry as recommended on the care label; if not, follow steps 6 and 7.

6. Soak it in hot water and powdered oxygen bleach for at least 8 hours or overnight (see the Soaking section on page 65) OR spray the garment with 3% hydrogen peroxide and allow it to air-dry.

7. Rewash and inspect before drying.

Watermelon

TYPE: Enzymatic

DIFFICULTY: Moderate

WHAT YOU WILL NEED: Clean towel and/or soft-bristle brush, all-purpose stain-remover spray (with the enzyme pectinase), powdered oxygen bleach or 3% hydrogen peroxide (as needed)

1. Wipe, rinse, or gently brush away any physical bits of the remaining stain with the towel or brush.

2. Tamp or pat in the all-purpose stain remover (the enzyme needed to break down the watermelon stain is pectinase) with the brush.

3. Allow this pretreatment to sit on the stain for 15 minutes.

4. Wash as recommended on the care label.

5. Inspect before drying. If the stain was removed, dry as recommended by the care label; if not, follow steps 6 and 7.

6. Soak it in hot water and powdered oxygen bleach for at least 8 hours or overnight (see the Soaking section on page 65) OR spray the soiled areas with 3% hydrogen peroxide and allow to air-dry.

7. Rewash and inspect before drying.

Wax

TYPE: Special

DIFFICULTY: Hard

WHAT YOU WILL NEED: Old clean towels, hair dryer, rubbing alcohol (isopropyl alcohol)

1. Gently brush and lift away any physical bits of the remaining stain with your hands.

2. Put a clean towel behind the stain and warm up the stain with a hair dryer. Once the wax has melted, blot the stain with a second clean towel and enough rubbing alcohol to cover the area of the stain.

3. Wash as recommended on the care label.

4. Inspect before drying. If the stain was removed, dry as recommended by the care label; if not, follow step 5.

5. Get this garment dry-cleaned. Dry-cleaning solvent makes wax stain removal quite easy.

HOW TO CARE FOR DIFFERENT FABRICS

When it comes to caring for different types of fabrics, understanding the unique needs of each material is essential for maintaining their quality and longevity. From delicate silks to sturdy denims, each fabric requires specific washing techniques and handling to keep them looking their best.

Plant Fibers

FABRIC EXAMPLES: Cotton, flax, hemp, jute, ramie, bamboo, sisal
GARMENT EXAMPLES: T-shirts, sheets, undergarments, towels, chinos

WASHING: Plant-based fibers can usually withstand aggressive wash cycles and higher heat; however, those cycles should be reserved for heavily soiled pieces. Gentle wash cycles paired with low temperatures will be more than enough for normally soiled garments and prevent your garments from prematurely fading and falling apart.

DRYING: Most of these fibers hold on to quite a bit of water, so they will usually take a while to dry. We recommend using low temperatures and long cycles to get a nice, even dry. Try removing your garments from the dryer when there are a few minutes left to avoid static and wrinkling.

IRONING: If your natural-/plant-fiber garments are wrinkled, first start with steaming. If that does not work, iron on a medium temperature.

BLEACHING: We highly recommend only using oxygen bleach on cotton, as chlorine bleach can alter the color of your garments. The only time you should be using chlorine bleach is if you have concerns about sanitization.

DRY CLEANING: Rarely should plant-based fibers require dry cleaning; however, if you have a tricky or hard-to-remove stain, give them a call.

Note: Hot water WILL fade your garments prematurely, so avoid using hot water on your plant-based fibers at all costs. If you need some extra cleaning power for your laundry loads, try adding powdered laundry boosters.

Animal Fibers

FABRIC EXAMPLES: Cashmere, wool, mohair, camel, alpaca, silk
GARMENT EXAMPLES: Knits, suits, blouses, undergarments, overcoats, jackets

WASHING: Some animal fibers can be washed at home and others cannot. This is dependent on the weave and garment type rather than the specific fiber. For example, most knit tops and sweaters can be cared for at home (see Handwashing on page 63), but items like wool suits and camel overcoats should be given to a professional. To wash animal fibers at home, use a detergent designed for handwashing animal fibers. The reason this is so important is that most of these detergents are "no rinse" products. These detergents purposefully leave behind conditioners on the fibers to protect them. Think of animal fibers like your hair; it's important to condition it to keep it soft, less tangled, and protected. These detergents should prevent your garments from pilling and feeling rough and scratchy.

DRYING: The best way to ruin an animal-fiber garment is to put it in the dryer. When caring for most* animal fibers at home, you must lay them flat and let them air-dry. Tumble drying animal fibers will cause mass shrinkage and hang drying will cause stretching (the weight of the water will stretch it out). We recommend laying a clean towel under your animal-fiber garment, rolling it up, giving it a squeeze to remove excess water, and then letting it air-dry on the same towel or a fresh, dry towel.

*Silk, which is technically an animal fiber, should be hung to air-dry.

IRONING: Iron the item inside out with low heat.

BLEACHING: You should never use any form of bleach on animal fibers.

DRY CLEANING: Dry cleaning is required for items like wool suits and mohair jackets, due to the complex nature of their construction. When in doubt, bring it to a dry cleaner and ask for their honest opinion on whether they should clean it or if it can be done at home.

Regenerated Fibers (Wood Pulp)

FABRIC EXAMPLES: Rayon, acetate (this type of fiber has been traditionally used as a substitute for silk)

GARMENT EXAMPLES: Shirts, blouses, dresses, skirts, scarves, garment linings

WASHING: Check the garment care label. Rayon and acetate trend to shrink if machine-washed. Many of these fibers are "dry clean only." If you want to wash rayon or acetate at home, we recommend handwashing only in cold water.

DRYING: Hang and air-dry only.

IRONING: Acetate requires an iron temperature of 290°F (143°C) and rayon 375°F (190°C). Again, check the garment care label for specific instructions. Steaming works well with these types of fabrics.

BLEACHING: Do not use chlorine bleach on these fibers. Oxygen bleaches can be used.

DRY CLEANING: Rayon and acetate generally can be dry-cleaned with great results.

Synthetic Fibers

FABRIC EXAMPLES: Polyester, nylon, spandex, acrylic, vinyl, microfiber

GARMENT EXAMPLES: Polyester, athletic wear, swimwear, outer jacket shells, leggings

WASHING: Synthetic fibers usually don't hold on to most water-based stains compared to natural fibers, due to their hydrophobic (water-fearing) tendencies; however, synthetic fibers cling to oils, due to their lipophilic (oil-loving) tendencies, which can promote odor-causing bacteria that thrive off body oil.

DRYING: If possible, air-dry just about every synthetic garment you own. These fabrics dry extremely quickly because they are designed to wick away moisture. Over-drying these fabrics will cause them to break down prematurely, which is especially true with spandex and stretchy clothing. Additionally, hard creases, which can be very hard to remove, can be caused from over-drying synthetic materials.

IRONING: If cleaned and dried correctly, there should be very few wrinkles or creases. But if you do need to iron them, we recommend ironing on a low temperature.

BLEACHING: Only use oxygen bleach. Chlorine bleach will not work to correct staining on synthetic fabrics.

DRY CLEANING: Most synthetic fabric garments can be cared for at home.

HOW TO CARE FOR SPECIAL ITEMS

Make sure to read the garment care label. If it says "dry clean only," then take a trip to the dry cleaner. If the label says "do not wash," you are risking the item by washing it, and you may ruin it.

Baseball Caps

The cardboard in the brim of these caps is the problem. Never machine-wash; you will destroy the brim. If the inside is greasy and/or yellowed, follow our instructions for removing "grease" stains (page 162), treating that area first. Then hand-wash (page 63) and air-dry. If any part is still yellow after handwashing, follow the guide for "sweat" (page 190), but skip the machine-washing step. Never dry in a clothes dryer.

Cloth Diapers

Dirty cloth diapers should be rinsed before washing them to remove any solid waste. Then you should follow our advice for "feces" on page 154 of The A-to-Z Stain Removal Guide, as there are specific steps and products that should be used to make sure that diapers are correctly sanitized during washing. Diapers need special care to remove and destroy harmful pathogens. Don't skip any steps when washing diapers at home.

For those who are unable to follow these washing procedures but want to use cloth diapers, there may be a diaper service in your area. These firms will pick up dirty diapers and replace them with clean, sanitized diapers.

Delicates

Lace, sheer fabrics, embellishments, boning, underwire in bras, and so on are prone to damage in routine washing. We recommend that if you are using the Delicate/Gentle cycle (page 59) on your washing machine, you should place your items in a mesh laundry bag (lingerie bag); this will protect the fabric during agitation and prevent other garments from snagging them. Wash in cold water with a mild detergent. The safest way to wash delicates, if you have the time, is to hand-wash them in your sink (see Handwashing on page 63).

Do not put these items in a dryer. Tumbling them could damage the fabric, underwire, or boning. They need to be air-dried and kept out of the sun to prevent fading. If you do not have a garment drying rack, you can place your items on a towel or over a hanger to dry. We have used our shower curtain rod at home to air-dry delicate items on hangers, and it has worked well.

Elastic

No matter what you do, elastic is going to break down over time from both use and the heat of drying. When elastic breaks down, it loses its elasticity and no longer stretches and rebounds. If you have a garment that has a lot of elastic, such as a shirred top or dress, follow the care instructions to the letter and do not dry in a clothes dryer (the heat from the dryer will cause the elastic to fail over time).

Graphic/Silk – Screened T – Shirts

You want to preserve the graphics for as long as possible unless you want your brand-new tee to look like a vintage shirt. Wash it inside out in cold water with a mild detergent on the Delicate/Gentle cycle of your washing machine. Air- or line-dry (in the shade). The more the tee gets tumbled in the washer and dryer, the more it will look vintage over time.

Jeans/Denim

We are going to "poke the bear" a bit with our advice. Some people never wash their raw denim jeans, as once they hit water, they are never the same. Indigo dye used on denim is very fragile, hence the reason jeans fade so quickly, even just by wearing them.

If you need to wash your jeans and want to preserve the color as much as possible, turn them inside out and wash in cold water on the Delicate/Gentle cycle with mild detergent, then air- or line-dry. Even using this technique, your jeans may shrink somewhat (no you did not gain weight!), but they should stretch out after a few wears. We have seen some jeans labeled "do not wash, dry clean only," and we would recommend following those instructions .

We have encountered some denim sites that advocate spraying jeans with vodka or popping them into the freezer to "clean" them. These techniques may remove odor, but they are not getting them clean. We have found that dry cleaning jeans preserves the color, and the fabric doesn't shrink as much.

Pillows

If your pillow can be washed (many cannot), use the Bulky/Bedding cycle on your washer. Pillows may pick up yellowing from perspiration and oil in our hair. If this is the case, you may need to soak it before cleaning (see Soaking on page 65). Use a mild detergent, and the Bulky/Bedding cycle will spin your pillow faster to remove excess water. If your pillow is down-filled, feather-filled, or cut foam–filled, you will need to get the clumps out. Dry on low and add dryer balls, clean tennis balls, or clean cloth sneakers to fluff up the filling. If you shake out your pillow a few times during the drying process, this will help with the clumping. Air drying doesn't work with clumpy pillows; you will need to use a clothes dryer. Note: Use the Soaking method on page 65 before drying if you are still unsatisfied with the color of your pillows.

Sneakers

Cloth sneakers, like Vans or Converse, can be machine-washed on a Delicate/Gentle cycle if they are super dirty, then air- or line-dried. All other sneakers will need to be cleaned by hand. There are too many mixed materials used in sneakers to recommend handwashing.

Swimsuits

Swimsuits need extra care, as they are exposed to salt water, chlorine, and sunscreen, all which can be damaging. After wearing your swimsuit, it needs to be washed and rinsed as soon as possible. Hand-wash or use the Delicate/Gentle cycle of your washing machine. There are detergents formulated for swimsuits, so that may be a good choice. Air-dry only. Note: Whatever you do, don't put your swimsuits away while still damp! This will cause mold and mildew problems.

Keep in mind that exposure to chlorine in some pools will cause bleaching of swimsuits. If you swim in a pool with chlorine, rinse your swimsuit in fresh water as soon as you exit the pool for the day. Also avoid sunscreen with avobenzone, as this chemical can cause yellow or brown stains to appear after washing. The only way to remove these stains is to use a rust remover. If possible, it's easier to use sunscreen that does not contain avobenzone than to remove these stains.

What Else?

We could write an entire book that gives advice on how to wash each and every garment you may ever encounter. Our advice to you is to read the garment care label and follow the advice. This label will tell you what temperature of water to use, if your garment can be dried (and what temperature to use), and if it can be ironed or steamed (see The Garment Care Label Guide on page 129).

INDEX

A

ammonia, 28, 29, 47, 192
athletic wear, 37, 38, 39, 77, 115, 199

B

baking soda, 28, 43, 45, 46, 48
bleach
    adding to washing machines, 55, 58, 61
    bleachable stains, 44
    bleaching agents, 25
    chlorine bleach, 29, 67, 196, 203
    garment care labels, 133
    oxygen bleach, 29, 65–66, 196, 199, 202
    "pens" and 49
    safety, 28, 47, 67, 198
    sanitizing with, 67, 196
boosters. *See* detergent boosters
borax, 28, 43, 45, 58
builders, 25, 43

C

chlorine bleach, 29, 67, 196, 203
Clean Club website, 16, 24, 28, 47, 126
clotheslines, 18, 78, 80–81, 99, 132
cold water
    Colors cycle, 60
    detergents and, 61
    environment and, 123
    garment care labels, 54, 131
    Hand Wash cycle and, 63
    jeans and denim, 202
    preference for, 62, 119
    stain removal and, 45
color
    bleeding, 68, 69
    chlorine bleach alternatives, 29
    fading, 102
    jeans and denim, 202
    oxygen bleach and, 133
    sorting by, 36–37, 105, 118
    tannins and, 143
    water temperature for, 60, 67, 131
community laundry rooms, 20, 21, 59

D

delicates
    dryers and, 39, 76, 77, 131

garment care labels, 54, 74, 130, 131
mesh laundry bags for, 37
sorting, 34, 36, 37
washing machines and, 59, 60, 63, 130, 201
denaturation, 43
detergents
    adding to washing machines, 56–58
    anti-redeposition agents, 25
    auto-dosing, 56
    bleaching agents, 25
    builders, 25, 43
    cold water and, 61
    cost differences, 24
    DIY recipes, 25
    dosing guidelines, 57–58
    eco-friendly detergents, 26
    enzymes, 25–26, 43
    fragrance, 25
    liquids, 26
    overdosing, 59
    pacs, 26, 27–28
    powders, 26
    recommendations for, 24
    sheets, 26
    sud sensors, 57
    surfactants, 25, 42
    washing machines and, 55
detergent boosters
    adding to washing machine, 55, 58
    ammonia, 28, 29, 47, 192
    baking soda, 28, 45
    borax, 28, 43, 45
    chlorine bleach, 29, 67, 196, 203
    favorite recipe, 45, 119
    oxygen bleach, 29, 45, 61, 65–66, 133, 96, 199, 202
    pH and, 45
    recipe, 45
    scent beads, 31
    vinegar, 29
    washing soda, 29, 45
drip drying, 74, 132
dry cleaners
    form air finishers, 109
    garment care symbols, 135
    guarantees from, 107
    hand irons, 110
    history of, 104
    Hoffman press, 108

hot head presses, 109
machines for, 105
necessity of, 102
need for, 102–103
pant pressers, 109
pressing machines, 107–108
process overview, 104–105
receipts, 110–111
reputation and, 111
reviews, 110
roller presses, 109
rush service, 109
shipping services, 111
shirt units, 109
solvents for, 104
spotters, 106–107
spotting boards, 107
stain removal, 106–107
sweater boards, 109
vacuuming, 108
wet-cleaning machines, 106
dryer balls, 31, 79, 81, 202
dryers
    control panel, 75
    cycle selection, 76–77
    delicates, 39, 76, 77, 131
    door, 75
    down and, 79–80
    drum, 75
    dryer sheets, 30–31
    garment care labels, 74, 88
    laundry rooms, 21
    lint filter, 75
    maintenance, 79–80
    minor odor removal, 99
    moisture sensors, 77
    troubleshooting, 79–80
    ubiquity of, 78
    wrinkles and, 78, 86
drying
    clotheslines, 18, 78, 80–81, 99, 132
    garment care labels, 88
    sorting and, 38–39
    temperatures for, 119
    wrinkle prevention, 119

E

environment
    laundry and, 123
    regulations and, 110
    water temperatures and, 123

enzymes, 25–26, 43, 46
extraction machines, 184

F

fabric care. *See also* garment
    care labels
    animal fibers, 197–198
    plant fibers, 196–197
    regenerated fibers, 198
    synthetic fibers, 199
fabric softener, 30–31, 55, 58,
    80, 146
folding
    mental state and, 123
    sorting and, 126
    surface for, 126
form air finishers, 109
front-loading washing machines,
    52

G

garment care labels. *See also* fabric care
    bleaching and, 133
    checking, 34
    dry-cleaning and, 135
    drying and, 74, 88, 131–133
    hand-washing and, 63
    hot water, 54, 131
    ironing and, 88, 134
    laws for, 68
    washing symbols, 130–131

H

hand irons, 108, 110
handwashing, 63–65
hanging, 94
health, 123
history, 16–18
hot head presses, 109
hot water
    environment and, 123
    garment care labels and, 54, 131
    oxygen bleach, 29
    sanitizing with, 67
    shrinkage and, 63, 66
    soaking in, 62, 65
    stain removal and, 45, 60
    whites and, 60, 62
hydrogen peroxide, 25, 47, 65, 133

I

"ink loads," 34
intimacy, laundry and, 124
ironing

distilled water for, 85
function of, 84
garment care labels, 88, 134
process overview, 88–89, 91
settings, 87
wool, 89

J

Jeeves, 11, 13–15, 119

L

labels. *See* garment care labels
laundromats, 21, 114
laundry
    author routine for, 119
    environment and, 123
    frequency, 114–116
    hacks for, 118
    health and, 123
    help with, 127
    intimacy and, 124
    longevity and, 123
    mental state and, 122–123, 127
    overwhelm and, 127
    reward for, 127
    routine for, 114, 119, 126
    schedule for, 126
    sleep and, 124
    squirt bottles, 118
    stains and, 115
    time management and, 114
    timing of, 114
laundry rooms, 20, 21, 114
line drying, 74
lint, 36

M

mechanical action, 27, 28, 53, 55, 61
mesh laundry bags, 27, 37, 76, 201
moths, 97

O

oxidation, 44, 65, 96
oxygen bleach, 29, 45, 61, 65–66,
    133, 96, 199, 202

P

pant pressers, 109
particulate stains, 43
"pen" products, 49
pockets, 35
pressing machines, 107–108
pretreating, 35

R

roller presses, 109

S

scent beads, 31
shirt units, 109
shrinkage, 63, 66, 69
soaking method, 65–66
socks, 37
sodium percarbonate. *See* oxygen bleach
sorting
    button handling, 35
    clothing stress and, 38
    color sorting, 36–37
    drying and, 38–39
    garment care labels, 34
    laundry sorters, 36
    "like items together," 36
    lint and, 36
    pockets, emptying, 35
    socks, 37
    time-savings with, 126
    zipper handling, 35
    special items
    baseball caps, 200
    cloth diapers, 200
    delicates, 201
    denim, 202
    elastic, 201
    graphics, 201
    jeans, 202
    pillows, 202
    silk-screened t-shirts, 201
    sneakers, 203
    swimsuits, 203
special stains, 44
spotters, 106–107
stains
    acrylic-based paint, 180
    animal fats, 136
    ash, 137
    avocado, 138
    away-from-home treatments for,
    48–49
    baby food, 139
    barbecue sauce, 140
    beer, 141
    beetroot, 142
    berries, 143
    betalains, 142
    blood, 144
    body odor, 145–146
    bronzer, 147

chocolate, 148, 174
coffee, 149
combination stains, 45
cranberry, 149
crayons, 150
curry, 151
deodorant, 152
dry cleaning process for, 106–107
egg, 153
enzymatic stains, 43
fabric softener and, 145
feces, 154–155
foundation, 156
fruit juice, 157
glue, 158
grass, 159, 160
gravy, 161
grease, 162
greasy/oily stains, 42
hot sauce, 163
impossible stains, 45–46
ink, 34, 164
ketchup, 165
kimchi, 166
laundry and, 115
lipstick/lip gloss, 167
mango, 168
maple syrup, 169
marker, 182
mascara, 169
meat drippings, 170
micellar water, 156
mildew/mold, 171
milk, 173
milk chocolate, 174
molasses, 175
moths and, 97
mud, 160, 176
mustard, 177
nail polish, 178
oil-based paint, 180
olive oil, 179
online resources, 47
online techniques, 48
oxidizable/bleachable stains, 44
paint (acrylic-based), 180
paint (oil-based), 180
paint (water-based), 180
particulate stains, 43
peanut butter, 181
"pen" products, 49
permanent marker, 182
pet urine, 183–184
pretreating, 35
product safety, 47–48

products for, 46
red wine, 185
rust, 186
salad dressing, 187
Sharpie, 182
smoke, 188
soy sauce, 188
special stains, 44
spotting boards, 107
squirt bottles for, 118
storage and, 95–96
sunscreen, 189
sweat, 190
tannins, 143
tea, 190
tips for, 45
tomato sauce, 191
tools for, 46
treatment timing, 48, 49
urine, 183–184, 192
vomit, 193
water and, 42
water-based paint, 180
watermelon, 194
water temperature and, 45
wax, 195
wine, 185
starch, 90
steaming, 84, 85
storage
    air circulation, 99
    cleaning for, 95
    freshness and, 99
    hanging, 94
    mending for, 95
    moths and, 97
    plastic protection, 97
    space for, 98
    stains and, 95
    vacuum sealing, 98
sud sensors, 57
surfactants, 42
sweater boards, 109
synthetic fabrics, 38, 199

T
temperatures. *See* cold water; hot water; warm water
top-loading washing machines, 52

V
vacuuming, 108, 184
vacuum sealing, 98

W
warm water, 54, 64, 131
"wash and fold" services, 21
washboards, 17

washing machines
    agitator, 53
    auto-dosing detergent, 56
    compartments drawer, 53
    components, 53
    control panel, 53
    cycle selection, 58–60, 61–63, 67
    delicates, 59, 60, 63, 130, 201
    detergent addition, 55, 56–58
    detergent dosing guidelines, 57–58
    detergent overdose, 59
    for dry cleaning, 105
    "dry clean only" items, 69
    fabric softener and, 55
    front-loading machines, 52
    garment care label and, 54
    hand test, 54
    history, 17, 18
    laundry pacs and, 28
    laundry rooms, 21
    loading door, 53
    mechanical action, 27, 28, 53, 55, 61
    optional product additions, 58
    post-wash inspection, 63
    process overview, 61–63
    product addition, 55
    sanitizing with, 67
    starting, 61–62
    sud sensors, 57
    top-loading machines, 52
    troubleshooting, 69–71
    tub, 53
    unwashable items, 54, 68
    wet-cleaning machines, 106
washing soda, 43, 45
wet-cleaning machines, 106
white garments
    detergent boosters for, 28, 29
    hot water and, 60, 62
    soaking method, 62, 65–66
    Whites cycle, 60
wool
    ironing, 86, 87, 89
    sorting, 34
    steaming, 85
worldwide laundry, 18–19
wrinkles
    drying and, 78, 86, 119
    ironing, 84, 86–89
    laundry sorting and, 37
    steaming, 84, 85

ACKNOWLEDGMENTS

We are incredibly thankful and fortunate to have the opportunity to write this book. There are numerous people behind us who made this possible. Thank you, all, for your support, encouragement, and belief in this endeavor.

We extend heartfelt appreciation to Lisa and Alix, the women who are the foundation of our family. To Alix, thank you for always supporting our creative endeavors and believing there was a way, even when it was often quite dark. To Lisa, we will never be able to express our gratitude for your ceaseless stoicism, never-ending support, and unconditional love. Thank you to all the supporters in our extended family who know how hard we've worked to get to this point in our careers.

Thank you to Erin Canning, our editor, and the entire team at Rock Point and The Quarto Group for taking a chance on us making a book outside their normal bounds. Your patience with respect to our seemingly endless research and scientific process is truly appreciated.

Our deepest thanks and appreciation to the academic community, scientists, and fabric-care experts who helped us with countless hours of experimentation, research, and fact checking to ensure the information in this book is as thorough and correct as possible. A special thank-you to our incredibly knowledgeable mentors, Iain Weir and Alan Spielvogel, who always answer our technical questions about fabrics, dry cleaning, and laundry when we are stumped.

Finding the time to write this book would not have been possible without our staff, both past and present, that make Jeeves New York the industry leader it is today. We thank you for your incredible efforts. To our partners, Victoria and Rich Aviles, your ceaseless efforts, support, and pursuit of perfection always enable us to operate at the highest level. In addition, thank you to the clients of Jeeves with amazing wardrobes, family heirlooms, and special cleaning projects that keep us on "top of our game" on a daily basis.

I (Zach) need to personally thank my dad, Jerry (Joel). Thank you for giving up an untold amount of weekends driving me around for Frisbee tournaments, trusting me with perpetuating the family business, and allowing me to experiment with my obscure obsession to turn your four decades of wisdom into content that everyone can learn from. I know you were skeptical at first but your willingness to give me a chance has given me the confidence and hopefulness to always want to achieve more.

Finally, dearest gentle reader, your curiosity and questions continue to inspire and elevate our craft. We hope you find this resource useful!

ABOUT THE AUTHORS

Zachary Pozniak grew up around the family business and formally entered the industry in 2018. Known to his one million+ TikTok, Instagram, and YouTube followers via his handle @jeeves_ny and for his lint-roller "microphone," Zach doses out laundry tips and tricks for everyone—from budget-friendly advice to behind-the-scenes looks at cleaning luxury garments. Zach started his formal training with a degree in mechanical engineering from Binghamton University. Shortly after, he moved from engineering to consulting in boutique hospitality and high-end residential construction. In late 2019, Zach was brought on at Jeeves New York to oversee customer service, operational management, and marketing. Besides his incredible social media outreach, Zach has contributed to features in the *New York Times'* Wirecutter, the *Wall Street Journal*, *Elle*, *Huffpost*, *Good Housekeeping*, and *New York Magazine*'s The Strategist, among others.

Jerry Pozniak, born and raised in Corona, Queens, started his dry-cleaning career in 1986 at his family's business, Cameo Cleaners of Gramercy Park, after graduating from the School of Visual Arts with a major in photography. The original plan was to help out the family business for a few years, but thirty-four years later, he is still thriving in the dry-cleaning industry. In 2010, he became the managing director and owner of Jeeves New York and has not looked back. In New York, Jeeves is regarded as "the" destination for luxury garment care and is a worldwide brand with locations in thirteen cities. Personally, Jerry has cared for garments that have been exhibited at the Louvre, the Cooper Hewitt, the Fashion Institute of Technology, and the Metropolitan Museum of Art. For five years, Jerry was solely responsible for the cleaning of the costumes for the Metropolitan Opera House. Jerry has appeared as a fabric-care expert on *Good Morning America*, *20/20*, and ABC News and has been profiled in the *New York Times*, the *Wall Street Journal*, the *Washington Post*, *Time Out New York*, and the *Robb Report*.